The Guitar

from the Renaissance
to the Present Day

The Guitar
from the Renaissance
to the Present Day

Harvey Turnbull

Charles Scribner's Sons
New York

To my sister Elizabeth, without whom much of the research for this book would have been impossible.

Copyright © 1974 Harvey Turnbull

Copyright under the Berne Convention

Printed in Great Britain
Library of Congress Catalog Card Number 72–9038
SBN 684–13215–x (cloth)

Contents

Contents

Music Examples

Plates 1 to 28 are between pages 56 and 57. Plates to 29 are 46
between pages 88 and 89.

Preface

In 1963 a music historian wrote of the early nineteenth century guitarists that they 'represented such a special clique of dilettantes, performers and composers (as they still do today) that they have made but a small mark if any on general histories of music'.[1] The present book grew out of the inadequacy of general histories of music to satisfy my own curiosity about the history of the guitar; incidentally, I hope that it goes some way towards showing that the bracketed comment in the above quotation is an unacceptable judgement. If the general histories were uninformative, a little research revealed that many of the specialist books were positively misleading in their promulgation of legends and misrepresentations of historical fact. No doubt this is the cause of the classic example of confusion that occurs in the fifth edition of *Baker's Biographical Dictionary of Musicians* (New York, 1958), according to which Giuliani died on 8 May 1828, but then managed to visit London in 1833 ... Happily this *faux pas* has been emended in the sixth edition of the *Dictionary*. A further feature of many of the specialist works, and one that is particularly objectionable, is their uncritical acceptance of any music written for the guitar as good, almost by definition; perhaps the guitar is unique in its power to inspire such an emotional approach.

The unreliability of much of the secondary material made recourse to primary sources a necessity, which in turn entailed an extensive research programme. Fortunately, the task has been eased by the appearance of reliable articles and theses, and my debt to these will be obvious. However, a number of relatively unexplored areas remain. As yet, a reliable comprehensive source of information on the music and a wide enough comparative examination of extant instruments are not available. Circumstances have not permitted the undertaking of the detailed research necessary to fill the gaps, and the instruments that have been examined have been described as they

[1] William S. Newman: *The Sonata in the Classic Era,* p. 93

I

are; no attempt has been made to place their various features in chronological order except where good evidence for this already exists.

It has been customary to begin histories of the guitar with a consideration of the lute-type instruments of Antiquity and the Middle Ages in an attempt to determine the origins of the guitar and to account for the appearance of the instrument in Europe. The problems involved in these questions are many and varied and, as a critical discussion of the theories that have been put forward and an evaluation of recent archaeological finds would demand much more space than that of one or two chapters, this subject matter has been omitted in the present book. The Renaissance has been chosen as a suitable starting point, as it is only from this period that one can consider the guitar in relation to its music. Although it is easier to achieve historical continuity from this time, even this comparatively late period is not without its difficulties, present in the many apparently contradictory statements about the guitar recorded by early writers. I have tried to reconcile these by proposing lines of development suggested by the various relationships in tuning and construction of the lute, the Spanish vihuela, the Italian viola da mano and the four- and five-course guitars.

The history of the guitar presents the researcher with a vast amount of material, and it was obvious that, if an unwieldy account was to be avoided, much of it would have to be omitted. Consequently I have concentrated on what seemed to me the most important aspects of the different periods and treated them in some detail. As a result, some sources are mentioned only to place them in context, while many minor figures, whose inclusion would have meant rather tedious lists of names, have been left out.

I am indebted to Dr. Laurence Picken, Fellow of Jesus College, Cambridge; to Graham Wade, Guitar Tutor in the Holland County Music School, and to Neil Dunlop, my former pupil, for reading my work in typescript; their comments and suggestions have been most helpful and have led to a number of improvements. However, I must claim the credit for any errors. I am also grateful to Mrs. Elizabeth Wells, Curator of Instruments in the Royal College of Music, London, and to Mr. Desmond Hill, of W. E. Hill & Sons, who made arrangements for me to examine the guitars in their collections. Jack Schuman, Head of the Art Reference Library in the Cleveland Mus-

eum of Art, Ohio, very kindly supplied me with photographs of the
interesting guitars in his collection.

The Hobby,   H.T.
Cambridge

Chapter 1

The Development of the Instrument (1):
The Vihuela and early Guitars

The variety of plucked instruments in use in Europe in the Middle Ages was extremely wide. By the sixteenth century, however, the number of forms was smaller; some had fallen by the wayside, while others had achieved universal acceptance. Sometimes perfection was attained, as was the case with the lute, but generally the instruments of the sixteenth century were to remain only until they in turn were supplanted by superior versions. In spite of this, they lasted long enough to establish a corpus of music that reveals the extent to which they were favoured. This was the situation with regard to the vihuela and the four-course guitar, ancestors of the modern instrument.

The Vihuela and the Viola da Mano

The vihuela was pre-eminent among instruments of the guitar class in Renaissance times. Although it is convenient to use the term *vihuela* to indicate one instrument, it was originally employed in a general sense, and specific instruments were referred to as *vihuela de arco* (a bowed form), *vihuela de peñola* (played with a plectrum) and *vihuela de mano* (plucked with the fingers). The first two names can be found in medieval sources, but the third has not been traced back further than the late fifteenth century.[1] In the sixteenth century, however, the plucked form had become so well established in Spain that *vihuela* alone was sufficient identification. It is true that Luis Milán uses the full form on the title page of *El Maestro* (1536), but the vihuelistas who followed him found this an unnecessary practice, and *de mano* did not appear in the titles of their books of music.

It will be convenient to begin a consideration of the vihuela by quoting Johannes Tinctoris, who in 1487 described an instrument:

invented by the Spanish, which both they and the Italians call viola, but the French the demi-luth. This viola differs from the lute in that the lute is much larger and tortoise-shaped while the viola is flat, and in most cases curved inwards on each side.

Tinctoris also comments that:

while some play every sort of composition most delightfully on the lute, in Italy and Spain the viola without a bow is more often used.[2]

It is not surprising to find a Spanish instrument in use in Italy, as at this time there was a taste for things Spanish there. This was the result of Spanish rule in Naples, and even the Borgias, as Jacob Burckhardt relates:

are no more Italian than the House of Naples. Alexander spoke Spanish in public with Cesare; Lucrezia, at her entrance to Ferrara, where she wore a Spanish costume, was sung to by Spanish buffoons.[3]

As in Spanish, the full Italian name for the instrument was *viola da mano*, and it is featured in Italian works of art from at least the first half of the fifteenth century.[4]

The outline of a waisted instrument with a sharply bent-back and curved peg-holder appears among the border illustrations of the first page of Francesco Landini's madrigal 'Musica son' (Plate 2). This is one of a number of fourteenth-century compositions gathered together in what is now known as the *Squarcialupi Codex*, after Antonio Squarcialupi (d. 1470), the Florentine organist, by or for whom the collection was made. Although it is not shown being played, it is reasonable to assume that this instrument represents a viola da mano, as it is placed between two plucked instruments, a lute and a mandore. The lack of detail in the viola is unfortunate, but the two lines at the bottom of the body, if they are not mistakes, may be significant. Tinctoris's comment that 'in Italy and Spain the viola without a bow is more often used' suggests that the bowed viola played an important role in the development of the plucked viola/vihuela, and in fact they had much in common. The fifteenth-century viol (Plate 2) had a guitar-shaped body, gut frets tied round the neck and the strings tuned to the intervals of the lute (fourth, fourth, major third, fourth, fourth). The most noticeable differences in the vihuela/viola da mano were the central rose and the strings attached to a bridge fixed to the table, features that are more suitable to a plucked instrument than soundholes in each side of the table and strings passing over a bridge to a tailpiece. The lines at the bottom of the Squarcialupi viola, in the form of a 'V', may represent a tailpiece, and thus indicate an instrument at a transitional stage.[5]

Two violas da mano appeared in a Portuguese bible illuminated partly in Lisbon and partly in Florence; they are shown being played, and the central rose is evident (Plate 4). The folio containing these border illustrations is the title page of Isaiah, one of seven illuminated opening pages executed in Italy; other opening page illuminations are in a Portuguese style. It has been suggested that the reason for this dual illumination is that the manuscript was written in Lisbon in the 1490s and illumination began shortly before the Jews were expelled from Portugal in 1496–97. Illumination was then continued in Italy, most probably in the workshop of Attavante degli Attavanti in Florence.[6]

From the same period comes a waisted instrument depicted in the hands of Apollo (Plate 5a). This appeared in Franchinus Gaforus' *Practica Musicae*, which was published eleven years after Tinctoris was writing. It is rather surprising to find the lute relegated to a subordinate position, particularly when a succession of lute books was to begin to appear in Italy in the opening years of the following century. However, the prominence given the viola da mano confirms Tinctoris's observations of what was fashionable in Italy. The backward-bent peg-box is obviously taken from the lute (Plate 6) as is the rose. The stringing is only vaguely indicated, but another illustration in *Practica Musicae* (Plate 5b), although with different waisting, clearly shows seven strings at the bridge, which might be the artist's way of indicating seven courses (that is, double strings; sometimes the top course was a single string, but it was still known as a course). One cannot always rely on early illustrations as far as the number of strings and their correspondence with the number of pegs is concerned. For example, the vihuela illustrated in Luis Milán's *El Maestro* (Plate 11), which *must* represent a six-course instrument, has only six strings and ten pegs. The viola da mano in the engraving by Marc Antonio Raimondi of the poet Achillini (Plate 7) also has only ten pegs, but seven courses are clearly indicated. This seven-course viola da mano has a rose like the lute's and the peg-box of the bowed viol.

The instrument played by the angel (Plate 8) is very similar to the Achillini viola. The number of strings at the bridge indicates a six-course instrument. It is one of the instruments played by a group of angels in Luca Signorelli's fresco 'Crowning of the Elect' (1499–1505) in the Cathedral of Orvieto, Italy. Again the viola occupies a prominent position, being placed above the other instruments. The viola in Cariani's *Gli Amanti* (Plate 9) helps establish this type as a generally employed instrument. It has five strings at the bridge which appear to become courses where they pass under the musician's hand, so we can accept it as a five-course viola.

The final Italian viola to be considered is most realistically portrayed and leaves no doubt about the number of courses (Plate 10). It appears at the foot of the painting *Madonna and Child with St. Anne* (1518) by Gerolamo dai Libri. It is being played by an angel who, together with a lute-playing angel, provides instrumental accompaniment to a third angel singing from a book of music. The juxtaposition of the two instruments reveals the lute to be somewhat larger than the viola, and their roses have the same design. The viola has eleven strings arranged in six courses, the first course having only one string. Other features of interest are the low position of the bridge and the extension of the table a little way into the fingerboard, which lies flush with it.

In spite of the viola da mano appearing so frequently in Italian iconography, no music was published for it in Italy; from this point of view the lute was the preferred instrument. There are, however, a number of literary references to the viola's use as an accompaniment to the voice,[7] seen in some of the illustrations of viols already considered (Plates 7, 8 and 10). Benvenuto Cellini's father, Giovanni, learnt the viol and flute in the 1480s and Benvenuto, who was born in 1500, reports hearing him singing and playing the viola on the occasion when he boxed his five-year-old son's ears to draw his attention to a salamander in the fire. Although 'da mano' does not accompany Cellini's references to the viola, it is generally agreed that the plucked instrument was meant; presumably the instrument was so well known that such identification was considered superfluous, as happened at a later date in Spain. Cellini's father was passionately keen on music and as well as a performer he was, according to his son, a maker of considerable skill, producing organs, harpsichords, violas, lutes and harps.[8]

The fact that the viola da mano was not prominent as a solo instrument in Italy may be accounted for by an early sixteenth-century comment by Paolo Cortese on its sound quality:

> *the Spanish lyre [probably the vibhuela] . . . its equal and soft sweetness is usually rejected by the satiety of the ear, and its uniformity is longer than it could be desired by the limits imposed by the ear.*[9] *(translator's brackets)*

However, a later source reveals that it did not completely die out. In his *Dialogo Quarto* (Naples, 1559), Bartholomeo Lieto Panhormitano discusses tablature and its applications in the context of the viola da mano and lute.[10]

That the real home of the vihuela was Spain, as suggested by Cortese and Tinctoris, is confirmed by the wealth of music published for it there in the sixteenth century; the Italian viola da mano players might well have used these sources as well as the lute tablatures. In Luis Milán's *El Maestro*, Orpheus is shown in a sylvan setting playing a vihuela of similar size to its Italian counterparts, differing only in the type of peg-holder and the amount of decoration on the table (Plate 11). The peg-holder is only slightly inclined; the lute's peg-box is at a right-angle to help establish the balance of the instrument, but this is not necessary on a guitar-type. A similar peg-holder can be seen on the only surviving specimen of a vihuela, now in the Musée Jacquemart-Andrée in Paris (Plate 12). As well as the unexpectedly large number of roses, the table bears a motif remarkably similar to that on Milán's vihuela.[11] Although the peg-holder can accommodate 12 pegs to hold the original six courses, the marks on the bridge space indicate that the instrument was later used as a five-course guitar; this is confirmed by the number of notches in the nut. A possible earlier bridge occupied a lower position, and it has been pointed out that these positions of the bridge establish vibrating lengths of the strings which would allow either nine or ten frets on the fingerboard.[12] It is quite a large instrument and, except for the width of the lower bout (the lower half of the body), 32·8 cm., and the depth of the body, 7·2 cm., it is larger than the modern concert guitar. But perhaps the most striking feature of this vihuela is the extent to which various parts are built up sectionally. The head, neck, back and side-walls are constructed from separate pieces of wood; in the head, neck and back the strips of wood are joined side by side, whereas the walls are composed of interlocking sections. A reference to this form of construction occurs in the *Examen de*

Violeros (1502), which includes *un vihuela grande de pieças* in the list of instruments a prospective candidate must be able to make.[13]

The vihuela's tuning and the style of the music it inspired have led a number of scholars to refer to it as a lute and talk about 'Spanish Lute Music'. Gilbert Chase has reacted strongly to this attitude and prefers to refer to the vihuela as a 'six-stringed guitar'.[14] This is understandable in the light of the instrument's obvious affinities with the modern guitar, but it becomes confusing when we learn that there was an instrument bearing the name of 'guitar' in the sixteenth century which led a very different life from that of the vihuela. Consequently it is advisable to retain the name 'vihuela' to identify this instrument of dual personality and reserve 'guitar' for its companion.

Four-course Guitar to Five-course Guitar

A consideration of extant specimens and representations of early guitars reveals that they were much smaller than the six-course vihuela. A further point of contrast is that alongside flat-backed guitars there existed guitars with backs built of curved ribs similar to those of the lute (Plate 6). This method of construction can be seen in the four-course guitar made by Giovanni Smit in Milan in 1646 (Plate 13). It is quite small, having a length of only 56·5 cm. An earlier instrument, the Belchior Dias five-course guitar in the collection of the Royal College of Music in London, shares the rounded back of the Smit guitar, but the fluting is more prominent (Plate 14). This instrument bears a label which reads: *Belchior Dias a fez em: Lxa nomes de dez^{ro} 1581* (made by Belchior Dias, Lisbon, in the month of December 1581). The open soundhole is not original; like all early guitars it would have had a rose. This was often sunken and generally of extremely delicate workmanship (Plate 21d). The overall length of the Dias guitar, 76·5 cm., makes it about three-quarters the length of the vihuela. The table, of very fine grain, is divided (the table on the Jacquemart-Andrée vihuela is made of one piece of wood) and is extremely delicate. The neck is set into the body in the typically Spanish fashion; it continues into the body and ends in a fork, the upper prong of which is joined to the table, the lower one to the back. This gives a much stronger joint than when the neck is simply dovetailed into an end block.[15] (Plate 47)

An early Spanish illustration from 1502 (Plate 15) shows an instrument with a small, slightly waisted body, five strings (presumably meant to indicate courses) and a peg-holder that seems to be of the viol type although its right-angled attachment to the neck recalls the lute; its pegs are laterally inserted. A later illustration, however, has the slightly inclined peg-holder of the Spanish vihuela with the pegs inserted from the rear (Plate 16a). The strings are very clearly shown arranged in four courses.

The illustrations of the four-course guitar outside Spain reveal only one which has the vihuela-type head. This is shown on each of the title pages of four books of tablature published in mid-century Paris (Plate 16b). The remaining French instruments (Plate 17) have viol heads, as does the German example (Plate 18).

An examination of the side-walls of these instruments suggests that in most cases their backs were flat, if judgement is based on the fact that the sides are shown to be parallel. An exception is the Stimmer guitar (Plate 18) where the side seems to be deeper at the waist. If this is compared to the three-quarter front view of the Dias guitar (Plate 45) the conclusion might be drawn that its back was rounded in a similar manner.

The bowed viola/vihuela development commented on earlier is an obvious source for the flat back. Equally clearly the round back was inherited from the lute. This is substantiated by Johannes Tinctoris, who also reveals a further influence of the lute on the guitar:

> *Furthermore, there is the instrument invented by the Catalans which some call the* guiterra *and others the* ghiterne. *It is obviously derived from the lyre [lute] since it is tortoise-shaped (though much smaller) and has the same stringing and method of tuning.*[16]

The lute's 'stringing and method of tuning' played an important part in influencing the variety of sixteenth-century guitar tunings. The late fifteenth century was a transitional time for the lute. It had started its European existence with four strings, tuned at the intervals of fourth, major third, fourth. Double strings (courses) were introduced in the middle of the fourteenth century to give greater resonance, and a fifth course was added a fourth *above* the top string. The final course was added towards the end of the fifteenth century; this time the addition was in the bass. The resulting intervals of fourth, fourth, major third, fourth, fourth were, as has already been pointed out, to be a feature of the viola and the vihuela as well. It is of interest to note that Tinctoris included the viola as well as the guiterra among instruments derived from the lute. However, the vihuela had each of its courses tuned at unison, whereas the lute had its three lower courses tuned at the octave above.

The Spanish four-course guitar in Plate 15a appeared just after the publication of *Orphenica Lyra* (1554) by Miguel de Fuenllana, which contains music for 'the four-course vihuela, which is called guitar'.[17] Juan Bermudo, writing in 1555, asserts that the four-course guitar could have two tunings: *a los viejos*, with the intervals fifth, major third, fourth, and *a los nuevos*, with the four courses corresponding to the inside four courses of the vihuela. He adds that the bottom course in this second tuning has the two strings tuned an octave apart like the lute or 'vihuela de Flandes'.[18] This establishes doubling at the octave above on the four-course guitar. A further tuning is recommended by Alonso Mudarra for one of his pieces in *Tres Libros de Música* (1546).[19] He suggests that a *bordon* is added to the fourth course, which results in octave doubling below. This practice existed outside Spain; the tuning in the instructions which preface the collection of pieces for four-course guitar by Pierre Phalèse (1570) has the bottom two courses doubled at the octave below.[20]

The dual influence of the lute and the vihuela on the guitar had far-reaching effects. The resulting strains of curved- and flat-backed instruments persisted until the lute went out of fashion in the eighteenth century. It would, of course, be quite natural for the guitar, primarily a popular instrument, to adopt features of the nobler lute and vihuela. Both were instruments of professional musicians, and their music, so often a feature of court life and aristocratic gatherings, gave them a much higher status than that enjoyed by the guitar.

The guitar was still undergoing development in the second half of the sixteenth century, when the four-course instrument fell out of favour and the five-course guitar became the established instrument. The addition of the fifth course was not a straightforward process; there were two types of five-course guitar in existence, which differed in the location of the major third in the interval pattern. Bermudo reveals that one type was present in the first half of the century:

We have seen guitars with five courses in Spain. The fifth course can be placed on this instrument for music which has a compass of seventeen notes or more. This music can easily be played on the guitar if the fifth *string is added a fourth above the first.*[21] (my roman)

Thus the instrument in Plate 15 might be regarded as a five-course guitar, although it is difficult to determine what sort of back it had because of the roughness of the drawing of the side. Bermudo does not comment on doubling, but a French source, an illustration from 1585 by Jacques Cellier of a four-course guitar with a description of its intervals below, also contains a tuning in notation for a five-course guitar; this has the major third between the third and fourth courses as in Bermudo's five-course guitar, and also shows the fourth course doubled at the octave above (Plate 19):[22]

Had this interval pattern become established, the addition of a further string a fourth below would have given the modern guitar its six strings tuned in the lute/vihuela order of intervals.

In his *Guitarra Española de cinco órdenes* (1596) Juan Carlos Amat gives the tuning established at the end of the century:[23]

The *segundas* and *terceras* are tuned at unison (*en una misma voz*) whereas the *quartas* and *quintas* have strings of different thicknesses tuned an octave apart. Amat directs the player to begin from the *terceras* and tune the thinner of the *quintas* to the note given on the second fret of the *terceras*; the thicker *quinta* is pitched an octave below. The *segundas* are tuned from the second fret of the *quintas* and the thinner *quarta* is made equal to the third fret note of the *segundas*; the thicker *quarta* is at the octave below. Finally, the *primas* are tuned to the second fret of the *quartas*. The Amat and Cellier tunings agree in the octave doubling, but disagree in the location of the major third. Amat's version is, of course, the source of the modern guitar's interval pattern; a further string a fourth below produces the intervals we are familiar with today.

The presence of these two five-course guitar tunings in sixteenth-century Spain suggests a solution to the controversy about who was responsible for the addition of the fifth course. A literary source,

Lope de Vega's *Dorotea*, gives the credit for this to the poet and musician Vicente Espinel, referring to his adding the *prima*. This is repeated by Nicolas Doizi de Velasco in 1640, who comments further that it was for this reason that the instrument became known as the *Spanish guitar* in Italy.[24] Later in the same century Gaspar Sanz wrote that:

> *The Italians, French and other nations added 'Spanish' to the name of the guitar. Formerly it had only four strings, but in Madrid Maestro Espinel, a Spaniard, added the* quinta *and from this it derived its perfection. The French, Italians and other nations, imitating ours, also added the* quinta *to the guitar and for this reason called it the Spanish guitar.*[25]

Juan Carlos Amat also claims the instrument with the addition in the bass as the one known as the Spanish guitar.[26]

It has often been pointed out that Espinel was not born until 1550 and that he is hardly likely to have been responsible for a practice that was a tradition by the time it was noticed by Bermudo in 1555. This is true if it is a question of the *prima* addition. However, the *quinta* tuning did not become established on the guitar until later in the century, at a time when Espinel could have been respnsible for the practice. The association of Espinel with a form of accompanied monody, Spanish sonatas,[27] lends further support, as the *quinta* instrument was ideal for this. An explanation of why the addition of a fifth course in the bass was referred to by de Vega and Velasco as a *prima* addition is offered by an early eighteenth-century Italian manuscript in the British Museum (Sloane 2686 f.16). The tuning of the five-course guitar is given as: aa dd gg B♮B♮ e♮e♮ with the numbers of the courses underneath. Surprisingly the lowest course is numbered 1, the highest 5. If this continues an earlier practice and was one that was followed by de Vega and Velasco, then the confusion is dispelled; the addition of a fifth string in the bass which established the 'Spanish guitar' was sometimes referred to as the *prima* addition.

A precedent can be found for the intervals of the *quinta* tuning in Miguel Fuenllana's *Orphenica Lyra* (1554), which includes a number of fantasias for a five-course vihuela. Its tuning corresponded to the bottom five courses of the six-course vihuela and consequently would not have included octave doubling. At this period one of the four-course tunings had octave doubling below. The disappearance of this practice must have been the result of the increased size of the later guitar, which meant a greater vibrating length. This, plus the extension of the compass downwards of the *quinta*, suggests that doubling at the octave below became difficult to manage and the doubling above of the four-course guitar that Bermudo compared to the lute won through.

The five-course guitar that emerged in the seventeenth century did so only after a complex period of development in which it was subject to many influences. Although it bore the marks of its subservience to the lute and the vihuela, it nevertheless asserted its individuality by refusing to become completely identified with either. This independence was eventually to give the modern guitar its separate identity.

Fretting

Early lutes, vihuelas and guitars shared one important feature that would have been of practical concern to the player; the frets, unlike the fixed metal frets on the modern guitar, were made of gut and tied round the neck. The number needed varied according to the complexity of the music to be performed. On the lute and vihuela ten or eleven were necessary; the guitar had about eight for plucked music and as few as four if it was simply a case of strumming chords. Naturally enough the performer would want to know how to arrange the frets, and to this end he could have turned to a number of sources for guidance. The variations in these guides reflect the transition from a tuning largely based on Pythagorean principles to one of equal temperament, according to which the frets of the modern guitar are positioned. In this process the fretted instruments played a most important part.

One such account was to be found in a mid-sixteenth-century source of uncertain authorship.[28] This contains *La manière de bien et iustement entoucher les lucs et guiternes*, which was printed in Poitiers in 1556. The inclusion of the guitar with the lute in the title is a concession to the enormous popularity it was enjoying in France at this time. The method of fretting is first given for a particular instrument and then in the context of using it for instruments of different sizes. In the former, a line equal to the distance between the nut and the bridge is marked on a 'well-planed and polished table'. A ninth part of this line gives the position of the second fret. The fourth fret is a ninth of the distance from this fret to the bridge, and a further division by nine from the fourth fret gives the sixth. The seventh fret falls at a third of the whole length and the fifth is at a quarter. The third fret's position is established from the fifth fret; it is an eighth of the fifth fret-bridge distance from it. A similar method is used to locate the first fret; it is found at an eighth of the third fret-bridge distance from the third fret. Similar rules are given for the higher frets, but the author comments that only seven are necessary. The resulting divisions are transferred to the instrument and the player is advised to mark the neck so that he can easily reposition the frets if they become dislodged.

These positions of the frets produce a Pythagorean sequence of semitones; that is, they are not all the same size. The simplest way of appreciating the difference is to compare these semitone sizes with the semitone in equal temperament in the cent system of measurement. The equal tempered octave (1200 cents) divides into twelve semitones of 100 cents. The Pythagorean semitones are 114 and 90 cents. Bermudo calls the larger of these the *mi* semitone and the smaller the *fa*. He also gives a fretting method which is similarly Pythagorean. He establishes frets: 2, 4, 5, 7, 9 and 10 to give the diatonic tones and the remaining frets are placed according to whether the semitones they provide are *mi* or *fa*; if the former, they are placed nearer the bridge, if the latter, nearer the nut.[29]

The difficulty that such systems give rise to on fretted instruments is that the same fret has to serve all the strings, and one will not be able to use all the notes. For example, on a four-course guitar where we are to imagine the tuning: G c e a, with the sixth fret forming a *fa* semitone, c sharp cannot be played on the bottom course; it can, however, be played on the third course at the first fret because this is a *mi* semitone.[30] To overcome this difficulty, Bermudo even advocates having two frets, one for *mi* and one for *fa*. The directions he gives for locating the *fa* fret are the same as those in *La manière* for finding the first and third frets. For the two frets, different thicknesses of gut are used so that when the strings are pressed down on the *fa* fret they will clear the *mi*.[31]

Bermudo put forward a more complicated fretting procedure for a seven-course vihuela so that all the semitones could be played. According to J. Murray Barbour this is close to equal temperament.[32] However, towards the end of the century Vicenzo Galileo provided an easier formula in *Dialogo della musica antica e moderna*

(Florence, 1581). He proposed the use of the ratio 18:17 to locate the frets on the lute: the first fret is at an eighteenth of the entire vibrating length, the second an eighteenth of the distance between the first fret and the bridge, and so on. This is not quite equal temperament as each semitone is only 99 cents, but it is an excellent approximation. Indeed, it sounds very well against fretting established by a complicated theoretical computation taking all the various factors into account.[33] This 'rule of the eighteenth' has dominated fretting on the guitar ever since Galileo; the modern maker uses a more precise constant which is slightly less than an eighteenth.[34]

There is no doubt that Galileo was formulating a practice that had arisen much earlier in the century. John Ward has concluded from an examination of the vihuela tablatures that no notice was taken of larger or smaller semitones; the vihuelistas wrote down their compositions for instruments the fretting of which yields equal semitones.[35] However, difficulties could arise. Nicolas Doizi de Velasco, although regarding the guitar as having equal semitones, relates how he overcame the harsh sounds of notes in one mode heard immediately after playing in other modes. He left the guitar for a while, and when he tried the offending notes on their own, they sounded all right. He also comments on the clash between fretted and keyboard instruments because of the different semitone sizes;[36] similar reports begin in the mid-sixteenth century, indicating the earlier leaning towards equal temperament by players of fretted instruments.

Makers and Instruments

Although the extant instruments from the sixteenth century are few in number, there are records of vihuela and guitar making which reveal that by this time it was a firmly established activity. Spain and Italy were the main centres for the vihuela, but there are isolated examples of the instrument travelling further afield. A representation from Nuremberg (Plate 20) is the work of Peter Vischer the Younger; it may not be indicative of the existence of the vihuela in Germany, however, as Vischer spent much time in Italy, and the representation may merely reflect a southern impression on the artist, given expression when he returned home. A French reference comes from the inventory of the Parisian instrument maker Philippe de La Canessière, which includes *troys guiternes dont une a unze cordes et les deux aultres petites*,[37] the eleven strings indicating a six-course vihuela. Finally there is the inventory of Henry VIII's instruments, which includes four *gitterons*, further specified as *Spanish vialles*, evidence of the vihuela's presence in England.

In spite of Spain being the home of the guitar, there is as yet little information on early makers there. However, the situation is different in France, where the tremendous popularity of the instrument is reflected not only in the amount of published music but also in the high production of guitars. François Lesure has provided fascinating details of the fortunes of the instrument there.[37] Lyons was the earliest centre, and one often comes across mention of a *guiterne de Lyon*. It was here that Gaspard Duyffoprucgar (Plate 17b) operated. An account of his legal difficulties reveals the name of another guitar maker – Benoist Lejeune. Apparently he had been offering guitars for sale which were copies of Duyffoprucgar's instruments and he even used his mark, for which offence he was imprisoned. Another maker, Philippe Flac, of German extraction, was producing guitars in Lyons from 1567–72.

Paris did not lag behind Lyons, and Robert and Claude Denis, father and son, constructed hundreds of guitars there in the second half of the century. It is in the course of the inventories of these makers, which span the sixteenth and seventeenth centuries, that one notices the gradual shift in spelling from *guiterne* to *guitarre*.

There are many more guitars from the seventeenth and eighteenth centuries, the legacy of makers throughout the countries of Europe, and information is more readily available. In 1608 another legal dispute brings to light the activities of a Flemish maker in Naples – Jean Heindrickx, or Giovanni di Enrico, as he was known in Italy. He is described as a maker of lutes, guitars, citterns and violins. Heindrickx reported at a Governor's tribunal that two violins and two guitars made by him 'in the Spanish style' had been stolen from him when he was in Rome. He had recovered them from the people the thieves had sold them to and was demanding restitution. The description of the guitars gives details of their decoration, which included inlay of flowers in ebony on the back, a check pattern on the sides and much ivory.[38]

Embellishment was to be a constant feature of guitars up to the nineteenth century and, in the earlier period, it is rare for the beauty of the wood to remain unspoilt. However, it is difficult to gain a realistic picture of the extent to which guitars were decorated. Many of the specimens we have owe their survival to the fact that they were cherished as works of art rather than as musical instruments, and less imposing examples may have been discarded when they fell out of favour. The fact that the guitar had a lower musical status also contributed to this state of affairs; the lute, though occasionally decorated, was generally left plain. Mersenne, writing in 1636, talks of the makers' practice of adding ornament and figures to the back and sides to enliven and enrich the four-course guitar,[39] and this is evident in the illustration he gives. Lavish decoration may, therefore, have begun in the sixteenth century, although the Dias guitar and the representations in engravings and paintings are pleasantly restrained. Later instruments, however, are often overburdened with inlay and scenes worked in ivory, ebony, mother-of-pearl and tortoise-shell. The main centres of production were France, Italy and Germany – again Spanish examples are scarce. In the following survey only the most important makers in each country will be considered.

In the seventeenth century a high level of construction was reached in France, where, in the second half of the century, the guitar achieved great popularity in court circles. The outstanding name is that of Voboam, and instruments by Alexandre, Jean and René Voboam have been preserved. A guitar dated 1641 by René Voboam is in the Ashmolean Museum, Oxford (Plate 21). Its proportions call to mind the drawing of a five-course guitar in Mersenne's *Harmonie Universelle* from five years earlier, which also has a star-shaped design for the rose; the measurements of the Voboam guitar are: overall length 93·7 cm, width 20·5–18·3–24·6 cm, depth 77–88 cm, vibrating length of the strings 69·6 cm.[40] The alternating strips of ivory and ebony which line the edge of the table are extended along the sides of the fingerboard. This is known as purfling; it is functional as well as decorative as it serves to protect the end-grain of the table. This particular pattern is frequently met on French guitars of the period. On this instrument it is also found round the rose and on the bridge; the practice of using the inlay pattern round the soundhole for bridge decoration is followed by a number of modern makers. The back and sides of this Voboam guitar are made of tortoise-shell.

A similar guitar by Jean Voboam, now in the collection of the Conservatoire de Musique in Paris, was made in 1687 for Mademoiselle de Nantes, Duchess of Bourbon, a daughter of Louis XIV. It still has the original case, decorated with fleur-de-lys and a coat of arms. It is handsome instruments such as these that were heard at Versailles; a second guitar by Jean in the same collection was for

Mademoiselle de Chartres, Elizabeth-Charlotte d'Orléans, another of Louis XIV's daughters. It dates from 1676.

Alexandre's reputation lasted long after the seventeenth century. An advertisement in the *Journal de Musique* for September 1770 offered 'an excellent guitar made in Paris by the celebrated Voboam in 1675'; the seller was Le Clerc, *luthier aux Quinze Vingts*.[41] One of Alexandre's guitars was taken from the house of the Marquis de Luyignan de Lezay when the aristocrats suffered the official removal of their belongings after the revolution. Although the list of instruments taken makes sad reading, the guitars included in it bear witness to the continued popularity of the instrument with the upper classes at the end of the eighteenth century.[42] Alexandre's name was still respected in the following century; an account of makers includes him with the comment that his guitars were much sought after.[43] However, in spite of his fame, little is known of him; he lived in the rue des Arcis, where he also 'made castanets to perfection'.[44]

Many of Alexandre's guitars are less ornate than those by the other Voboams; this is true of the instrument by him in the collection of W. E. Hill and Sons in London (Plate 22). It is dated 1652 and, although it is too fragile to be handled, one can see that the sides are made of wood, the only decoration being a double line inlay. The instrument alongside it may be the work of Jean-Baptiste Champion, as it is similar in appearance to a guitar by him in the Museum of Fine Arts in Boston, USA;[45] if it is, it can be assigned to the end of the eighteenth century, as the Boston Champion guitar is dated *c.* 1800.

A French guitar that has acquired romantic associations is the so-called Rizzio guitar, originally in the Donaldson Collection and now in the Royal College of Music in London (Plate 28). It was featured in *Musical Instruments: Historic, Rare and Unique* (1888) by A. J. Hipkins, who said of it:

> *The apparent age of the guitar would agree with a supposed gift of it from Mary Stuart to Rizzio, and the fleur-de-lys might connect it with the French or Scotch Royal Families; but this slender suggestion of the fleur-de-lys, to which the guitar owes its special interest, unsupported by other evidence, is scarcely sufficient to uphold the fascinating attribution. Mr. Donaldson, however, informs me that this instrument was bought in Scotland, nearly forty years ago, from an old family that had possessed it or generations with this tradition of its former ownership.*

David Rizzio was Mary's secretary, and as he was murdered in 1564 this would make the guitar a sixteenth-century instrument if it belonged to him. Its measurements: overall length 93·5 cm, width 21·5–19–25·6 cm, depth 8·4–9·6 cm, string length 69·2 cm, make it similar in size to mid-seventeenth-century five-course guitars. Its purfling, the use of tortoise-shell strips and the design of the rose recall the guitar made by René Voboam. The Dias five-course guitar (1581) has overall length 76·5 cm, width 16·5–14·5–20 cm, depth 4–6·5–5 cm, string length 55·4 cm, and the many representations of the earlier four-course guitar reveal equally small instruments. Plate 28c shows the 'Rizzio' guitar between the Dias guitar and seventeenth-century guitars and the difference in size is immediately obvious. Consequently it is much more likely to have been made by one of the Voboams than a sixteenth-century maker.

Many other ornately decorated five-course guitars were made in France during the seventeenth and eighteenth centuries. They varied in colouring and motifs, often achieving great splendour. A further decorative practice, favoured by German makers, was the inlay of scenes depicting the hunt or other themes. This can be seen on the *chitarra battente* by Jacobus Stadler (1624) now in the London Hill collection (Plate 23). The *chitarra battente* had a curved, ribbed back like that of the round-backed guitar, but it had metal frets and strings that passed either over or through the bridge to be attached to pegs on the bottom of the instrument; a further difference was that the table formed a rise at the bridge instead of being completely flat. Played with a plectrum, it was used for accompaniment. The Stadler *battente* is not very deep but often *battente* bodies are very bulky. This is the case with another *battente* from the London Hill collection (Plate 23d). The 15 pegs on this instrument are for five triple courses. Three strings to a course could also occur on guitars; Michel Corrette describes a method of stringing with five courses tuned at unison, the fourth and fifth courses having an extra string tuned at the octave above. Such instruments with 12 strings were called *Guitarres à la Rodrigo*.[46]

Similar hunting scenes to those found on the Stadler instrument appear on other guitars, for example a guitar in the Royal College of Music collection (Plate 28c), which is thought to be of South German or Italian origin, and this style of decoration is a feature of some of the guitars built by Joachim Tielke of Hamburg, 15 of which are known.[47] A six-course guitar by him, dated 1693, is now in the

Victoria and Albert Museum collection. Evidence for the early use of a six-course guitar occurs in Joseph Friedrich Bernhardt Caspar Majer's *Neu-eröffneter Theoretischer und Praktischer Music-Saal* (Nürnberg, 1741); this must not be confused with the later six-course guitar as the tuning given by Majer is: d a d' f ' a' d".[48] The marquetry on this guitar is extremely elaborate. As well as classical scenes the back, sides and neck are crowded with flowers and foliage, echoed in the rose surround. Putti chasing animals appear on the back, and the head has a delicately carved putto and foliage in ivory (Plate 24). A five-course guitar by Tielke in the Royal College of Music rests content with floral design. The six-course instrument is quite large (overall length 105 cm, width 25–21–30 cm, string length 72 cm) when compared with the five-course (overall length 89 cm, width 19–16–23 cm, string length 63cm).

The names of Matteo and Giorgio Sellas dominate the seventeenth century in Italy. Active in Venice in the first half of the century, they produced many lutes and guitars, their instruments revealing a variety of decorative features. The back of the guitar by Matteo Sellas now in the Victoria and Albert Museum collection (unfortunately the front has been converted to a *chitarra battente*) is elegantly veneered in a zig-zag pattern of ivory and tortoise-shell (Plate 25). The neck is delicately inlaid in a design which is repeated on another guitar in the same collection but with the ivory and tortoise-shell interchanged. This positive-negative technique was even extended to the decoration of complete guitars to create a matched pair.[49]

A *chitarra battente* by Giorgio Sellas now in the Ashmolean Museum is more ornate. Dated 1627, it has mother-of-pearl panels on the head and fingerboard, and grotesque figures on the neck which continue along the sides. The same scene is on a neck by Giorgio in the Victoria and Albert Museum and also appears on a guitar in the Fitzwilliam Museum, Cambridge (Plate 26). The back of the Fitzwilliam Museum guitar is composed of ivory ribs, so delicate that they are translucent. The appearance of common features of decoration on guitars indicates either a common source of origin of the instruments or at least a centre of production of the features themselves. Early guitars generally present a wide range of decoration, and the complexity of the work involved in their production is expressive of the leisurely age that was their background.

After so much decoration it comes as a surprise, and perhaps a welcome one, to view the simple elegance of a guitar made by

Antonio Stradivarius. He is, of course, well-known as a superb violin maker, and his undoubted craftsmanship and appreciation of wood are evident in his guitars. Two of his five-course guitars are known, one in the Conservatoire National in Paris, the other in the Ashmolean collection (Plate 27). The restrained decoration serves to enhance the lines of the instrument and the beauty of the wood. The depth of the body is surprising, progressing from 9·5 cm, at the upper bout to 10·5 cm at the lower, measurements that would not be out of place on a modern guitar. Another comparison that can be made with the modern instrument is the position of the twelfth fret; the vibrating length of the strings of the Stradivarius guitar, 74·1 cm, and the length of the neck, 36·2, allow the twelfth fret to be placed almost at the point where the neck joins the body. This is unusual on five-course guitars; the modern twelfth fret position did not become standard until the early nineteenth century. The date of this Stradivarius guitar has generally been regarded as 1680, but David Boyden has suggested that the final digit is a badly formed eight.[50]

Although the seventeenth and eighteenth centuries were generally a quiet time for guitar making in Spain, the advances made there towards the end of the eighteenth century more than make up for this seeming lack of interest. These advances were to culminate in the modern concert instrument and they will be discussed in Chapter 4, when various features of the five-course instrument will be considered in the context of the changes apparent in the transition to the early nineteenth-century six-stringed guitar.

Chapter 2

The Sixteenth Century:
The Vihuela and the Four-Course Guitar

The Vihuelistas, their Music and Technique

Spain's 'Golden Age' is well represented in the music of the vihuelistas. Alongside compositions in traditional forms stand works that betray foreign influence. The vihuelistas were innovators in two important respects: in the cultivation of variation technique and in accompanied solo song. They are men of the Renaissance in their concern with things classical; the very titles of some of their books – *Orphenica Lyra, Libros del Delphín, Sylva de Sirenas* – indicate this in recalling classical myths. As well as giving permanence to their music – and how much music has been lost through not being written down? – the vihuelistas were greatly interested in the transmission of their art. They gave an account of technique and went to the trouble of arranging their works in a progressive order, sometimes signifying their level of difficulty. This concern surely indicates that, as well as providing music in court and aristocratic circles, the vihuela enjoyed a domestic existence and, for a while, had a place in Spanish life comparable with that of the lute elsewhere in Europe.

This regard for the amateur music-maker is well shown in the title of the first of the books devoted to the vihuela, Luis Milán's *El Maestro*, which was published in 1536; it followed the appearance of books of lute music in Italy, Germany and France earlier in the century. No collections devoted to the lute were published in Spain; the vihuela output of seven books spanned 40 years, the series being brought to a close by Esteban Daza's *Parnaso* in 1576.

Luis Milán is the best known of the vihuelistas, as we have more details of him than of the other vihuelistas, who have mostly left little more than their books of music. Born towards the end of the fifteenth century, Milán was a favourite in the court of Germaine de

Foix and the Duke of Calabria at Valencia, and his publications, both literary and musical, were inspired by its manners and culture. His first book, *Libro de motes de damas y cavalleros* (1535), depicts the rather frivolous pastimes that were part of court life. A later work, *El Cortesano* (1561), is a portrait of the ideal courtier, which, like similar sixteenth-century treatises, sets out what is socially acceptable. The better known *Book of the Courtier* by Baldassare Castiglione is an account of civilized pursuits in Italy, and no doubt the Duke of Calabria was partly responsible for similar fashions in the Spanish court. In this milieu, music played no small part, and in *El Maestro* we have a record of vihuela pieces which must have been heard at many a gathering in the court. It is, however, more than a collection; it is arranged in an order necessary for a complete beginner to acquire the desirable art of playing the vihuela.

In the Prologue Milán tells us he is self-taught, having always been very keen on music. He dedicates the work to King John III of Portugal, but, although he received a pension in return for the dedication, there is no evidence that Milán ever visited the country. Milán rather charmingly likens *El Maestro* to a precious stone which would lose its value if he were to keep it. He extends the analogy and relates the story of the philosopher who throws the stone into the sea. Swallowed by a whale, it is found in its dead body and taken to the king. The philosopher is content as it is now in its rightful place and its value is realized. So with *El Maestro* which, in being sent to Portugal, enters the 'sea of music'.

The Introduction contains practical directions for the performer (or should one say student?), although it is assumed that he has sufficient knowledge of singing to be able to follow a rhythm; that is, he should understand *compas*, the beat, and *mesura*, the value of the notes. Tuning the vihuela entails choosing strings of the correct gauge. For a large vihuela, the *primas* (the strings for the top course) should be thicker than those for a smaller size instrument. These are to be tightened to as high a tension as they can stand, pitch thus being determined by practical parameters. The other strings are tuned roughly from the top and checked by comparing unison and octave sounds. Accuracy was achieved either by adjusting the tension of the string or shifting the fret slightly.

Milán continues by explaining tablature. This was the system used to notate music for fretted instruments and was in use until the eighteenth century (Plates 30 and 31). In a simple way it can still be seen in the method of indicating chords in modern popular music. Its essence is that the pitch of the note is not directly given; it indicates where the player must place his fingers to achieve it. Consequently it is an easier way of arriving at the same end. There were different systems in use which, however, had many points in common. The strings were indicated by horizontal lines, and the frets were shown by numbers or letters. If numbers were used, o indicated an open string, 1 the first fret, and so on; if letters, a, b, c etc. served the same purpose. Milán's tablature differs from that used in the later books by having the top line indicate the top course. In Milán's case the highest line corresponds to the highest sounding string. The popularity of the second method rests on the physical correspondence between the lowest line of tablature and the highest sounding string when the instrument is in playing position. The values of each note or chord thus indicated is shown above the six lines, and each *compas* is marked by a bar line which, therefore, does not serve the same purpose as a modern bar line as it simply marks off one beat.

The Introduction concludes with an outline of the contents; the work is in two parts, the first containing music for a beginner, the second for the more advanced player. Milán comments that the music for the beginner is easy – in this way, he will not become discouraged. This interest in the beginner is carried on in some of the other vihuela books. Alonso Mudarra (*Tres Libros de Música en cifra para Vihuela*, 1546) opens his work with a number of fantasias marked either 'to develop the hands' or 'easy'. Miguel de Fuenllana (*Orphenica Lyra*, 1554) uses 'F' and 'D' to indicate easy and difficult pieces and Enríquez de Valderrábano (*Silva de Sirenas*, 1547) has three grades.

Milán is credited with providing the earliest tempo indications. These occur in the section devoted to *tañer de gala*, which is concerned with alternating fast and slow passages. Chordal sections (*consonancias*) are to be played slowly and the scale movements (*redobles*) quickly. The right hand techniques used for scales are those of *dedillo* and *de dos dedos*. The first is done with the index finger alone, while the second involves either the thumb and first finger or the first and second fingers striking the strings in an alternating movement. Mudarra gives specific signs for fast, medium and slow tempi and suggests that *dedillo* be used when playing from the top string to the lowest, while *de dos dedos* is better for the reverse movement. Fuenllana provides the most extended account of technique. He advises the beginner to play very slowly and carefully, and even for more advanced performers, delightfully described as those 'with hands', he avoids extremes in advocating that they go neither too quickly nor too slowly. On fingering he comments on the difficulty of using *dedillo* cleanly; he recommends the use of alternating thumb and index as better on the thicker strings but considers that the first and second fingers give greater perfection in both speed and clarity. Elsewhere in Europe the use of thumb and first finger only was common practice in scale playing; the use of the first and second fingers is met for the first time with the vihuelistas, and it was not until the early years of the seventeenth century that it was generally employed.[1]

These restrictions to the thumb and first two fingers are a consequence of resting the little finger of the right hand on the table; this can clearly be seen in the illustrations that show performance on the lute, vihuela and guitar (e.g. Plates 6, 11 and 18). This right hand position was to remain the standard approach until the nineteenth century. It limits the use of the third finger which, even in a free position, is very weak as it is physically dependent on the second and little fingers.

An important section in Fuenllana's introduction is devoted to *tañer con limpieza* – neat, or clean, performance. If an open string occurs within a chord and it should not be sounded, it can be damped by the thumb if it lies next to the string the thumb plays. A more important point reflects the inability of tablature to represent a polyphonic texture. When the realization of the music demands held notes against quicker moving voices, Fuenllana warns that the fingers should not abandon the long notes. To this end it might be necessary to locate the phrase in a higher position so that all the notes lie under the fingers. One very often comes across a similar practice on the modern instrument.

In spite of these points of contact the vihuelistas were not directly connected in terms of master-pupil relationships. Indeed, Luis de Narváez (*Los Seys Libros del Delphín de Música*, 1538) was completely unaware of Milan's work published two years earlier, although Mudarra makes reference to his predecessors. With the exception of Diego Pisador (*Libro de Música de Vihuela*, 1552), the vihuelistas were professional musicians in royal or aristocratic houses. In referring beginners to the best performers, Bermudo specifically mentions Mudarra, a canon in the Cathedral of Seville, Narváez, who was in

27

the service of Philip II, Fuenllana, in the service of the Marquesa de
Jarifa, and Anrique (Valderrábano), in the service of the Count of
Miranda. His list of excellent performers also includes vihuelistas
who left no music: Martin and Hernando de Jaen from Granada and
Lopez, musician to the Duke of Arcos.[2] Bermudo also praises Fuenllana's skill, which the player demonstrated to him, in improvising on
a vihuela with one of the courses raised or lowered a tone.[3] Another
method of distuning (*destemple*) was to raise or lower one of the
strings forming the third or fourth courses. Bermudo singles out Luis
de Guzman as a proficient executant on such a distuned vihuela;
sometimes the distuned string was avoided in performance, but
sometimes both strings were struck, the distuned string being
stopped to form a consonance with the tuned string.[4] Guzman's fame
had lived on after his death. He was killed in the sea battle at Naples
in 1528, and the report of his death is obviously by a writer who
appreciated music, to judge from his priorities:

> *There died on this day . . . Luis de Guzman, who was the greatest player*
> *of his time on the vihuela, and other important gentlemen and captains of*
> *infantry.*[5]

One aspect of vihuela practice not dealt with in the books of music
themselves, although they contain many examples of it, is intabulation – the art of rendering notation into tablature. The performer
would have found this necessary, as the price of books of music was
high. Spain lacked printing houses that specialized in music publishing, and the production of a book of tablature was therefore expensive. Bermudo is fully aware of the difficulties and offers helpful
advice. After furnishing the necessary technical details, he warns the
novice against being too ambitious; he should ignore fantasias until
he has gained experience. Bermudo recommends the beginner start
with *villancicos* and *musica golpeado* (strummed chordal music with all
the voices together); these can be managed without much difficulty.
The next stage is to tackle the *villancicos* of Juan Vásquez and the
works of Baltasar Tellez, which Bermudo thinks suitable as they are
graceful, easy to sing, with dissonances that sound well on the
vihuela, and their range is not too wide. He then moves on to the
masses of Cristóbal de Morales and the music of foreign composers
such as Josquin des Prez; finally, the music of 'the excellent Gombert', left to the end as it is most difficult to set on the vihuela.[6]

Intabulations first appear in Narváez (all Milán's pieces are his own music) and are a regular feature of the later collections. The material is used either as a faithful representation of the original in its entirety or a section may be taken to serve as the basis of a composition. The vihuelistas' choice reveals a response to foreign influence, and the music absorbed shows a sensitivity to both religious and secular music. One important stimulus was from the north:

in order to show their admiration for the ecclesiastical art of the Flemish and French composers, the Spaniards, in writing their Masses or when compiling their collections for organ or vihuela, based their works upon religious pieces of the French-Netherland school, chiefly on those of the masters of Charles V's chapel or of the French royal house, or transcribed these pieces for instruments.[7]

Narváez's third book contains sections of Masses by Josquin, and in the following book the religious mood is sustained with variations on the hymn melodies *O glorioso domine* and *Sacris solemniis*. Mudarra continued this practice by using Mass sections for his parody fantasias. Motets were also featured and in Valderrábano there is a greater number of composers whose works were borrowed: Philippe Verdelot, Nicolas Gombert, Adrian Willaert and Jacques Arcadelt appear as well as the inevitable Josquin. Vocal works by Josquin, Gombert, Willaert and Morales appear in Book Four in versions for two vihuelas.

Secular music was by no means ignored. Narváez's third book also includes French songs and the very beautiful *Mille regretz*, Josquin's *chanson*, which is sub-titled by Narváez 'The Emperor's Song', the Emperor being Charles V. Italian influences are evident in Mudarra, his *canciones* recalling early Italian madrigals which, together with his *sonetos en italiano*, settings of sonnets by Petrarch and Sannazaro, help revive the fashion started by Luis Milán, who also set Italian texts to vihuela accompaniment.

Villancicos and *romances* are included in all the collections. This is hardly surprising, as with them we are brought firmly back to Spanish soil. These forms already had a long and distinguished history prior to their cultivation by the vihuelistas, reaching back to the Middle Ages. The *villancico* was of popular origin, its refrain-stanza development of a narrative becoming shortened when taken over by the musicians.[8] Its themes were varied, but generally love was the dominant topic of interest, and its attraction was universal. Milán gives two versions of his *villancicos*; the first enjoins the singer to *hacer garganta* – 'use the throat', that is, improvise ornamentation, while the second gives running passages to the vihuela. His textures are basically chordal, while his followers produce a more polyphonic setting.

The *romances* began life as medieval epic poems, passed on orally as a means of broadcasting heroic deeds and events of historical significance. A later development was the outcome of the Moorish wars which gave rise to the *romances fronterizos* (border ballads). The subject matter of these verses contrasts sharply with that of the *villancico* and consequently evokes a more solemn musical setting. Like the *villancico*, however, the *romance* enjoyed popularity at all levels of society, and, again, adaptation was necessary for musical ends, which resulted in the *romances* becoming much shorter.

Milán includes four *romances*, *Durandarte*, *Durandarte* being his finest. The first part is the popular tune, while the music of the second part enlarges on the closing phrase of the first. The later vihuelistas varied the manner in which they treated the ballads, sometimes incorporating instrumental introductions. A feature of the tablature in the songs is the inclusion of the melody in the vihuela part, either by a dash, as in Mudarra, or isolated red numbers as, for example, in Valderrábano. There has been some controversy as to whether these should be played on the instrument. J. B. Trend thought this would be 'a positive insult to a good singer',[9] but generally it is reasonable to assume that they would have been included.[10]

One of the medieval *romances*, *Conde Claros*, originally ran to 206 lines. By the sixteenth century it had emerged as a purely instrumental form, with a theme short enough to invite many variations. To quote J. B. Trend once more; 'the variation form seems to have arisen in Spain through the necessity for relieving the monotony of the lute-accompaniment during the recitation of a long *romance*'.[11]

Example 1 : Narváez, *Conde Claros* Theme

Narváez extends this theme through 21 variations. The later vihue-listas also found it attractive, and the number of variations reached 74 in Valderrábano's second set. Narváez's sixth book also contains variations on the *Romanesca* theme:

Example 2: Narváez, *Romanesca* Theme

Known in Spain as *Guárdame las vacas* (look after the cows for me), this theme was also used by Mudarra, Valderrábano and Pisador. The outside influences on the vihuelistas were mentioned earlier; the technique of variation they instigated reversed the process as musicians elsewhere began to follow their precedent. It became a favourite form of instrumental writing in England, where it was known as divisions on a ground, but its value was generally felt.

The remaining instrumental forms found in the vihuelistas' collec-tions are also of great interest. The *fantasía*, which started life based on polyphonic vocal forms, is a constant means of expression with them. It is in his fantasias that Milán indicates *tañer de gala*; his fan-tasias are sometimes imitative, more often harmonic in their move-ment, betraying less sophistication than those of his followers. Narváez makes much greater use of imitation, a device to be found in the other vihuelistas up to Valderrábano and Fuenllana, with whom the polyphonic texture gives way to a more diffuse style, the voices being treated independently. In a different style is the exciting *Fantasía que contrahaze la harpa en la manera de Luduuico* (Fantasia that imitates the harp in the manner of Luduvico) by Alsonso Mudarra. The second half contains the comment: 'from here to the end there are some dissonances; if you play them well, they will not sound bad', a reference to the false relations that add greatly to the delight of the work.

Dance forms occur in the *pavana* and *gallarda*, but they do not form a significant part of the vihuelistas' repertory. Milán's six *pavanas* are deservedly popular; their clear-cut phrases and strongly chordal flavour make them easy to listen to. The first of Mudarra's two *pavanas* is based on the tune known in England as the 'Spanish paven' and used by Cabezón under the title *Pavana Italiana*. This and the two variation sets on the *pavana* by Valderrábano are really folia variations, the form that was later to become known as the *Folies d'Espagne*. It is echoed in Pisador's *Pavana muy llana para tañer* (Pavane that is very easy to play) and was to figure, often only with the harmonies, in the strummed chord books of the seventeenth-century guitarists. Mudarra includes a *gallarda* – the only time this occurs in the vihuela books.

The vihuela was a short-lived instrument, and it is remarkable that so much was achieved in such a short space of time. Its splendid music makes it difficult to understand why it disappeared in the latter part of the sixteenth century. The facile answer has been that it was replaced by the guitar, but this was no real replacement as the guitar inspired no comparable literature. It is also difficult to argue that other forms of music brought about the demise of the vihuela. It had much in common with the lute and this continued to flourish; it was just beginning its English life and was still thriving in France and Italy. The fact that the lute survived for so long, its decline in the eighteenth century brought on itself through its ever-increasing complexity, suggests either that the vihuela was not as responsive an instrument and failed to inspire musicians of the calibre of the lutenists or, failing that, that there were no more vihuelistas in Spain of the stature of the early masters. Whatever the reason, the vihuela gave way to the five-course guitar, but before its fortunes are followed, its direct predecessor, the sixteenth-century four-course guitar, should be considered.

The Four-course Guitar in Italy and Spain

The earliest published music for the four-course guitar appeared in Mudarra's collection of vihuela pieces (1546). Three years later Melchiore de Barberiis' *Opera Intitolato Contina* was published in Italy; after the works for the lute four *fantasias per sonar sopra la Chitara da sette corde* were added, the 'seven-stringed guitar' being, of course, the four-course instrument. The repertory in Spain and Italy in this period is completed by the guitar pieces in Fuenllana's *Orphenica Lyra*. It is significant that these works were included in collections devoted in the main to the vihuela and the lute; no single volume solely dedicated to the four-course guitar was published in Spain or Italy in the sixteenth century. From this one might infer that there was a public for music on the guitar that was more interesting than strummed music, but not one sufficiently large to warrant complete collections. The guitar's more respectable cousins, the lute and the vihuela, were more of an attraction to the serious amateur.

Melchiore de Barberiis was an outstanding lutenist in a city noted for its lutenists – Padua. 'Fantasia' is too grandiose a title for his guitar pieces; their style is closer to that of dances. Fewer directions for performance are given to them than to the lute pieces. The rather simple texture is managed by an alternating thumb and first finger movement, the dot under a number indicating the first finger (Plate 30c).

The Spanish pieces for guitar are more ambitious. Mudarra wrote six works, comprising four fantasias, a pavane and a version of *Guárdame las vacas*. The first fantasia is for a guitar tuned *al temple viejo*, the remainder *al temple nuevo*. Bermudo gives details of the distinction; he says that the old tuning differs from the new only in that the bottom course is a tone lower, giving a fifth instead of a fourth between the two lower courses. Further, the old tuning is more suitable for 'old romances and strummed music than for modern music', and when ciphering good music on the guitar, the new tuning is used.[12]

Unlike Barberiis, Mudarra produces fantasias more worthy of the name. Pieces in a simple chordal texture give way to works where consideration has been given to the movement of individual parts. Within the more limited compass of the guitar, themes are taken over by different voices. Perhaps the most interesting of Mudarra's guitar pieces is the *Romanesca II: O guárdame las vacas*. The splendid set of variations produced by Narváez on this theme has already been mentioned; Mudarra also wrote a set for the vihuela which is equally attractive. The guitar version allows comparison of the resources of the instruments; on the vihuela the variety of movement provides a more interesting texture that involves the listener to a greater degree.

The final source of four-course guitar music in Spain is Book Six of Fuenllana's *Orphenica Lyra*. Fuenllana composed nine pieces in all; six fantasias, the romance *Passeavase el Rey Moro*, the villancico *Covarde cavallero* and a setting of *Crucifixus est*. Except for the romance, Fuenllana labels them 'easy'. The fantasias make use of imitation, generally in three voices, sometimes four. The subject of the romance was popular with the vihuelistas; Narvaez and Pisador provided settings, and Fuenllana's version for guitar, although a simple two-part accompaniment, well sustains the sombre mood of the sadness of the Moorish King as Granada is wrested from him.

In the works for the four-course guitar published by Mudarra and Fuenllana no difference in technique is indicated; they are to be approached in the same spirit as the works for the more favoured instrument. It would be fair to regard this small collection as an adjunct to the main business of establishing a repertory for the vihuela.

The Four-course Guitar in France

The mid-century position of the four-course guitar in France was very different. The scene here is well set by the author of *La manière de bien et justement entoucher les lucs et guiternes* (1556), who relates that 'for the past 12 or 15 years, everyone has begun to play the guitar, with the lute almost forgotten', and to such an extent that 'you will find more guitarists in France than in Spain'. This is certainly borne out by the amount of music published there for the guitar. Between 1551 and 1555 nine books of tablature appeared, five from Adrien le Roy and Robert Ballard, three by Guillaume Morlaye and one by Simon Gorlier. The le Roy and Ballard collections have been known for some time, but the others were discovered only recently by François Lesure in the Vadianabibliothek, the town library of St. Gall in Switzerland. Obviously, with this number of publications, it is no longer a case of minority interests being served, as in Spain and Italy, but of satisfying an enthusiastic demand.

The four-course guitar compositions by the vihuelistas reveal an honesty of purpose. When we turn to the first book of tablature for the instrument to appear in France, we might well suspect that its publication was prompted by commercial interests. From the observations of the author of *La manière* it is clear that by the mid-century the guitar had quite a following. It is to this public that Simon Gorlier, described in the title of his book as *excellent joueur*, directed *Le Troysieme Livre . . . mis en tabulature de Guiterne* (1551). The dedication that prefaces the work is nothing more than an apologia. He has issued the work, not because he prefers the guitar to other instruments, but in honour of antiquity. He talks of the instrument's limitations and remarks that the works he has composed are according to its capacity. These 'compositions' are, in fact, intabulations of *chansons*, and Gorlier's apologetic attitude appears again in a preface to *La Bataille*, one of Clement Janequin's descriptive *chansons*:

> *such a small instrument (I mean 'small' in both senses of the word) does not merit the labour I have devoted to it. My excuse is that I have done it to give the reader pleasure and he must, therefore, take it in good part.*

Little is known of Gorlier. One reference that is not to his credit is the description of him by a Genevan musician, Loys Bourgeois, occasioned by their public dispute, as 'a poor musician who, although versed in Mathematics and Greek, knew nothing of the practice of music'.[13]

In the same year Adrien Le Roy's *Premier Livre de Tabulature de Guiterne* appeared. It is wider in scope than Gorlier's book, and the repertory is extended by two attractive *fantasies*, obviously meant for the more advanced player, and a number of dances – *pavanes* and *gaillardes*, *almandes* and various types of *branles*, *simple*, *gai* and *de Bourgogne*. These were very popular in the sixteenth century, and directions for their performance could be found in Thoinot Arbeau's *Orchésographie*, which describes the suitability of the *branles*:

> *Musicians are accustomed to begin the dances at a festival by a* Branle Double, *which is called a* Branle Commun, *and afterwards they give the* Branle Simple, *then the* Branle Gai, *and at the end the* Branles *which are called* Branles de Bourgogne, *and others which some call* Branles de Champagne. *The order of these four kinds of* Branles *is governed by the three types of people who take part in a dance. The old people gravely dance the* Branles Doubles *and the* Branles Simples, *the young married ones dance the* Branles Gais, *and the youngest of all dance the* Branles de Bourgogne. *And all those who take part in the dance acquit themselves as best they can, each according to his age, disposition and agility.*[14]

Of practical interest to performers was another publication by Le Roy, this time a tutor: *Briefve et facile instruction pour apprendre la tabulature a bien accorder, conduire, et disposer la main sur la Guiterne*

(1551), a further edition appearing in 1578. An English translation of Le Roy's work appeared in 1568, published by James Rowbotham, under the title *The breffe and plaine instruction for to learne the Tablature to Conduct and dispose the hand unto the Gitterne*. Unfortunately there are no known copies of these editions of this work, but it has been proposed that in compiling *Selectissima elegantissimaque, Gallica, Italica, et Latina in Guiterne Ludenda Carmina* (Louvain and Antwerp, 1570), Pièrre Phalèse borrowed Le Roy's instructions, which he included in his collection as a 'lucid and useful method'. The rules give an account of tablature and the manner of stringing and tuning the guitar, which has the two lower courses doubled at the octave below. A total of 3,600 copies has been estimated for the three lost editions.[15]

In 1552 three more books made their appearance. Le Roy issued his *Tiers Livre*, similar in content to his first, while the other two were by Guillaume Morlaye, who, in the title of his *Premier Livre de Chansons, Gaillardes, Pavannes, Bransles, Almandes, Fantasies* is described as a *joueur de Leut* (lute). He was probably a pupil of Albert de Rippe, a noted lutenist and teacher, but among his less praiseworthy activities was an interest in the slave trade in Senegal and the Antilles.[16] Morlaye's books have an international flavour. His *Premier Livre* includes *La Romanesque Gaillarde*, which, however, by the time *Orchésographie* was published, seems to have lost popularity, as Capriol could say:

> *When we gave our* Aubades *at Orleans we always played on our lutes and guitars the* Gaillarde *called* La *Romanesca. But to me it has come to seem stale and trivial.*[17]

Morlaye's *Quatriesme Livre* also contains a Spanish echo in the *Conte Clare*, which finds a double place in this collection; one version is for the guitar while the other is one of the pieces for cittern included at the end. An English intrusion in his *Second Livre* (1553) is the *Hornepipe d'Angleterre*, while from Italy comes Melchiore de Barberiis' first fantasia, which appears in this collection as a *Branle*.

Two *fantasies* opened Le Roy's first book; Morlaye followed this precedent in his three collections. The two that open his fourth book bear the title *Fantasie d'Albert*, the Albert being Albert de Rippe. The largest number of fantasias to be found in one book is six, composed by Grégoire Brayssing. Brayssing was born in Augsburg (his dates are not known) and had left Germany after the defeat of Frederick,

the Elector of Saxony, at the Battle of Mühlberg in 1547.[18] He settled
in Paris, where the *Quart Livre de Tabulature de Guiterre* published by
Le Roy and Ballard in 1553 was devoted to his pieces. Brayssing's
book contains no dances, but, as well as the fantasias, there are intabulations of the usual *chansons* and also several psalms. Le Roy's
fifth book, which contained *chansons*, mainly by Jacques Arcadelt,
appeared in 1554, and the French publications for the four-course
guitar are brought to a close by Le Roy's second book (1555), which
consisted of *chansons en forme de voix de ville*. In these last two books
the melodic parts are given in mensural notation.

Thus, in the short span of four years, nine books of tablature were
devoted to the four-course guitar, five from the publishing house of
Adrien Le Roy and Robert Ballard, two available at the next-door
premises of Robert Granjon and Michel Fezandat and, when their
partnership broke up, the remaining two, Morlaye's second and
fourth books, by Fezandat in association with Morlaye.[19] Their contents are largely intabulations of *chansons* and dances, providing a
body of music that is neither technically nor musically very demanding on the performer. As the examples show, their easy flowing
melodies phrased in clearly defined sections would have given them
an immediate appeal.

Example 3: Guillaume Morlaye: Book One, f. 28v. Allemande

The following *Gaillarde* became widely known. It was taken up in
England, where it was often referred to, in a variety of spellings, by
Elizabethan writers. In *Much Ado about Nothing* (Act II, Scene 1)
Shakespeare has Beatrice remark to Hero:

> *wooing, wedding, and repenting, is as a Scotch jig, a measure, and a cinque-
> pace: the first suit is hot and hasty, like a Scotch jig, and full as fantastical;
> the wedding, mannerly-modest, as a measure, full of state and ancientry;
> and then comes Repentance, and, with his bad legs, falls into the cinque-
> pace faster and faster, till he sink into his grave.*

Example 4: Guillaume Morlaye: Book One, f. 19v. *Gaillarde Les Cinq Pas*

The restricted range of the four courses of the small sixteenth-century guitar inevitably resulted in a harmonically limited style, evident in the contents of the books, but which probably did not diminish the popularity they enjoyed with the amateur performer. Daniel Heartz well sums up the situation:

> *The reinforcement of the two lowest courses at the octave below on the guitar, as on the French cittern, may help explain why the arrangers for the two instruments were little troubled by the $^6_4$ chords and sixth chords that*

infest their books – not that the $\frac{6}{4}$ chords are eliminated thereby, yet the added weight of sound in the bass register seems to attenuate their effect. In order to eliminate the rootless chords – a consequence of the restricted range of the instrument – it would have been necessary to transpose to higher keys, that is to say, to higher positions, thus imposing a difficulty on the player that is not at all in keeping with the social ends for which the books were intended.[20]

Many of the pieces fall within the first five frets, which on the small sixteenth-century guitar meant that the left hand did not need to move. The distance between the nut and the fifth fret on the Dias guitar, string length 55·4 cm, is 13·85 cm, according to the fretting rules of *La manière*. This is roughly equivalent to the nut to *fourth* fret distance, 13·4 cm, on a modern instrument with string length 65 cm. Thus, a chord such as the one that begins the eighth 'bar' of Morlaye's intabulation of *Plus le voy de beaucoup estimé* (*Le Premier Livre*, f. 5), which has the first finger on the second course at the first fret, the second finger on the third course at the second fret and the little finger on the first course at the fifth fret, would have been quite easy on the sixteenth-century guitar; on the modern instrument it is just manageable, but uncomfortable as the fingers must achieve a greater span than that of the natural four frets.

A more ambitious use of the instrument is revealed in some of the more extended pieces, the *fantasies*. Morlaye's are somewhat rambling; those by Brayssing and Le Roy are more attractive, in particular the two by Le Roy, which feature imitative and sequential passages and, in the first, a compass that reaches the eleventh fret.

Example 5: Adrien Le Roy: Book One.
First Fantasia (beginning)

The extent of the movement in these calls for a well practised guitarist and they form a marked contrast with many of the shorter pieces.

It has been suggested that the fashion for the guitar in France was set by royal circles,[21] and as early as 1530 the guitar had elevated connections. Ryckaert de Mont, described as a 'ghyterneur, suivant le mode espagnole', was in the retinue of the Emperor Charles v.[22] In England the small guitar was probably in use from the mid-century. In 1550 Sir William Petre paid six shillings for a *gyttron*[23] and an inventory of the goods of Leonerde Temperleye (1577) includes an old *syttrone* and a broken *gyttrone*.[24] The guitar should be distinguished from the English gittern, which had enjoyed widespread use in the Middle Ages. The Warwick Castle gittern, now in the British Museum, is a sole survivor of this class and it, too, features in the sixteenth century; tradition has it that it was presented to Robert Dudley, Earl of Leicester by Elizabeth I, and a plate on the instrument carries the arms of both. However, it is the newcomer from abroad that is featured as one of Leicester's interests in the portrait of him in the Bishop's Bible (1568).[25] A pavan and galliard for the four-course guitar appear in the Mulliner Book (*c.* 1560),[26] and the Lord Braye MS, compiled about the same period, also contains pieces for guitar.[27]

The Phalèse collection mentioned earlier provided the guitarists of the Netherlands with the mid-century French repertory, as it was largely composed of pieces from Le Roy's books. Later Northern interest is manifest in a manuscript group of pieces from the early seventeenth century.[28] Written on a five-line stave with the top line crossed out, they include *La Franchina*, which uses the tune of *Que la bella Franceschiana*, also featured in Luis Milan's fifth pavane.[29] A four-course guitarist is portrayed playing from tablature by Joos van Craesbeeck (1606–52) (Plate 29), but we are now on the periphery of four-course guitar activity and in the century that belongs to its successor, the five-course instrument.

Chapter 3

The Baroque:
Era of the Five-Course Guitar

Juan Carlos Amat and the Spanish Guitar

The published repertory for the vihuela and the four-course guitar was the zenith of instruments that extended back at least to the fifteenth century. They were succeeded by an instrument that was to last until the latter half of the eighteenth century, and in the course of its active life it gave rise to compositions which reveal that it, too, inspired a cross-section of musical society. Unlike the situation in the sixteenth century, however, the balance is tipped in favour of a very simple, popular style, and only occasionally do we meet a more ambitious approach which resulted in music that still has appeal today. The new era is heralded by Juan Carlos Amat's little treatise *Guitarra Española de cinco órdenes* (The Five-course Spanish Guitar) in the closing years of the sixteenth century. It was a popular work; it was reprinted throughout the life of the instrument it advocated.

The abandonment of the more refined vihuela was witnessed, most sadly, by Covarrubias,[1] who comments:

This instrument has been highly regarded until the present time, and has had most excellent musicians, but since guitars were invented, those who devote themselves to a study of the vihuela are small in number. It has been a great loss, as all kinds of plucked music could be played on it: but now the guitar is no more than a cow-bell, so easy to play, especially rasgueado,[2] there is not a stable lad who is not a musician on the guitar.

And in the entry under *Guitarra* he goes so far as to say that 'it has caused much damage to music which previously was played on the vihuela'.

The style that gave Covarrubias cause for complaint is to be found in *Guitarra Española*, which first appeared in 1596.³ Amat was not a musician by profession but a doctor, as is shown by his other works, which are mainly on medical subjects. Consequently it is not surprising that his book on the guitar describes a style of performance that does no more than enable its practitioners to strum a sequence of chords.

The aims expressed in the title are to teach the reader how to tune the guitar, play rasgueado, all the natural chords and those 'b mollados' (that is, major and minor chords), and to use these chords in accompanying a song. After giving the tuning (see above p. 13) Amat continues by explaining what he means by *punto*, which is a chord containing bass, alto and soprano. There are twenty-four of these: twelve major and twelve minor. In Chapters Three and Four a detailed description of each one is given to enable the reader to finger them on the guitar. Amat also points out where the root, third and fifth of each chord are to be located; the chords are distributed across the five courses according to the principle of which notes are available, so the root of the chord is not always the lowest note. Chapter Five gives a table that shows the location and fingering of the chords arranged in the cycle of fifths (Plate 31a). The upper part of the circle, designated N, represents the major chords, the lower, B, the minor chords. Each division has five boxes, which represents the strings, the outer ring of boxes indicating the fifth course. The numbers within the boxes stand for the frets, with the fingers used to stop down the strings shown by the letters a, e, i and o, which indicate the first, second, third and fourth fingers respectively.

Chapter Seven is concerned with the application of these chords. Amat compares them to a painter's palette; just as the painter chooses the colours he needs to depict a scene, so the player selects the chords to perform *vacas, passeos, villanos, italianas, pabanillas* and other forms. He gives the harmonic basis of the *paseo*, which consists of the chords of the tonic, subdominant and dominant with a return to the tonic, and for the *vacas*, which has the harmonies of the *romanesca, Guárdame las vacas*, in tabular form with the sequences spelled out in all keys. The guitarist can thus easily accompany other instruments.

Accompanying the voice is the subject of the following chapter, and again a table is given to make everything as simple as possible. Amat's concern is to enable the guitarist to select the correct chords using the bass of a part song. Once he has decided on the key he wants to use, the performer, following Amat's principles, can select the appropriate chord at a glance.

The approach expounded by Amat has been considered at some length as it occupies an important place in the history of the guitar. The importance is two-fold: Amat's book gives official recognition to a style of performance that was a long-established tradition at the end of the sixteenth century, and the principles it contains were to dominate the Baroque guitar to a greater or lesser extent. Mention has been made of the continued popularity of Amat's treatise; in his *Instrucción de Música sobre la Guitarra Española* (1674) Gaspar Sanz paid his respects to the doctor, and his work was copied by Andrés de Sotos in 1764 (*Arte para aprender con facilidad y sin maestro . . . la guitarra de cinco órdenes*) and reprinted as late as 1784.

The Spanish Guitar in Italy

There are very few Spanish sources in the new style immediately following the appearance of Amat's book. The Spanish guitar thrived in Italy, and the seventeenth century saw a steady stream of publications for what was obviously a very popular instrument there. In the early years of the century books devoted to the *Chitarra alla Spagnuola* appeared in Rome, Venice, Naples and Milan. Another term was *Chitarriglia*, which was opposed to *Chitarra* by, for example, Carlo Calvi, who, in his *Intavolatura di Chitarra e Chitarriglia* (Bologna 1646), relates that the *Chitarra* has proper tablature whereas the *Chitarriglia* only has chords. He says, however, that some of the *suonate* can be played on both, so the distinction may be simply one of style, although the diminutive might indicate a smaller instrument.

The Italian books used a chord system similar to the one set out by Amat. It was to become universally known as the 'Italian alphabet' and first appeared in Girolamo Montesardo's *Nuova Inventione d'Intavolatura per sonare li balleti sopra la Chitarra Spagnuola, senza numeri e note* (Florence 1606). 'Without numbers and notes' reveals that the player is not to be burdened with the disciplines of tablature or notation; it is sufficient to learn the series of chords by heart and play these when indicated. In place of the numbers used by Amat, capital letters are used to indicate the chords (Plate 31b); there are no musical relationships in the series of chords, and it has been suggested that the order may have been determined by the frequency of use of the chords.[4] It is not known if Montesardo used Amat's work, but the earlier system was forgotten when the Italian system became popular; indeed, Amat himself uses the letters to indicate the chords in later editions of his work.

The new style became established very quickly, the guitar pushing itself forward to feature alongside the harpsichord and *chitarrone* in the titles of publications. Vincenzio Giustiniani comments in his *Discorse sopra la Musica de suoi tempi* (1628):

> *Furthermore, the Spanish guitar* (chitarra alla spagnola) *came into favour at the same time throughout Italy, especially in Naples, and it seems almost as though the guitar and theorbo have conspired to banish the lute altogether. In this they have succeeded, just as the Spanish fashion in clothes prevails over all other fashions in Italy.*[5]

At first the guitar was reserved for less serious songs, those of a frivolous nature, but the distinction was lost; Nigel Fortune comments on 'the practice of providing every song with letters for the guitar, even when, as in more serious songs, they were wildly inappropriate (in the same way do the publishers of the popular sheet-music of today pepper their pages with tablature for the ukelele)'.[6]

In spite of some resistance a procession of simple books began to appear. Initially they were solely concerned with the alphabet and rasgueado technique, and this was so widely known that some books of verse appeared accompanied by the chord letters alone.[7] No punteado tablature was featured; the early seventeenth-century Italian books offer a number of dances only, simply presented as a progression of chords, to be played in a rasgueado technique, the right hand varying the up and down strokes according to the instructions given.[8] Benedetto Sanseverino refers to this method of sound production as most suitable for the guitar; to play the instrument in lute fashion would be to take from it 'its own natural and ancient style'.[9] There are further directions for performance in Giovanni Ambrosio Colonna's *Intavolatura di Chitarra Spagnuola* (1673):

> *The intelligent Maestro can choose his time to carry the hand well and sound with grace and modesty, playing now soft, now loud, in the true Spanish and Napolitan manner.*

The softening would have been achieved by playing between the rose and the neck, advice given by Pietro Millioni 'for greater swetness'.[10]

The Italian publications of strummed dances reveal more than any-thing else the true nature of the sixteenth-century life of the guitar. Strummed music had been noticed by Bermudo, and as he considered it old in 1555, it can be concluded that the chordal style persisted throughout the sixteenth century. Accompanied song was popular with the vihuelistas, and Milán's compositions reveal a pronounced chordal style. Although art music had been spasmodically influenced by popular undercurrents, the full effect of this force was not felt until the early seventeenth century. Also the short harmonic for-mulae that were the bases of the forms in the guitar books helped in the transition from the polyphonic style and modal theory to the major-minor system. As Richard Hudson has concluded as a result of a study of the Italian guitar books:

> *During the early years of the seventeenth century a number of different sources contribute to the gradual development of tonality . . . . certain tonal elements had long existed in the realm of popular music. The particular type of popular music most prevalent in Italy at this time was the music of the Spanish guitar. Furthermore, composers of serious art music incorporated into their works some of the forms that had originated in guitar literature. Both Praetorius and Gibbons present* zarabande. *Monteverdi identifies a vocal piece as a* ciaccona *and on another occasion indicates an improvised* passacaglio. *Frescobaldi composes* partite *on the* ciaccona, *the* passa-caglio *and the* folia, *as well as on some forms of probable Italian origin, such as the* monica *and the* ruggiero. *Major-minor tonality certainly resulted from many forces acting in a great historical evolution, and the modes and chord-rows of guitar music seem to have been a part of that complex musical development.*[11]

Without the development and interest of melodic movement, the many passacaglias, chaconnes, folias and other dance forms in these books must have palled after a while. Taken from their natural setting as a means of accompaniment, their sparse musical content could scarcely have satisfied Colonna's 'intelligent Maestro' for very long. Consequently a more complex tablature was devised, one that could include more ambitious musical thinking. This resulted in a mixture of the alphabet with the longer established tablature to indicate single notes (Plate 31c), which first appeared in *Il primo, secondo e terzo libro della Chitarra Spagnola* (c. 1629), the work of Giovanni Paolo Fos-carini, who styled himself *L'Academico Calignoso detto il Furioso* –

'the obscure Academician known as The Furious One'. Foscarini did not introduce the new style without some reserve, though; in the introduction to his collection he declares, commenting on the *sonate* called *pizzicato*, that 'they are more suited to the lute than to the guitar', and more or less apologizes for their inclusion by referring to them as 'embellishment'.

After Foscarini further collections featuring mixed tablature appeared. These include the works of Giovanni Battista Granata (publications 1646–80) and Domenico Pellegrini (1650), but perhaps the most attractive music of seventeenth-century Italy came from Ludovico Roncalli, whose *Capricci Armonici sopra la Chitarra Spagnola* appeared in 1692. His suites of dance forms often contain movements of great charm, such as the Prelude of Suite No. 7 in D minor and the Gigue of Suite No. 1 in G major. Variation technique, so splendidly established by the vihuelistas and followed by the four-course guitarists, is met again in the elegant Passacaglia of Suite No. 9; it contrasts sharply with the strummed passacaglias that opened the century.[12]

The Italian guitarist who dominated the second half of the seventeenth century was Francesco Corbetta (Plate 32), who anticipated nineteenth-century trends by travelling widely as a virtuoso performer. His effect was felt mainly in Paris and London, where he initiated a craze for the instrument in royal circles.

The Spanish Guitar in France and England: Francesco Corbetta

The reception given the Spanish guitar in France in the early part of the seventeenth century was, to say the least, not particularly warm. An attempt to popularize the style of performance that had been taken up so enthusiastically in Italy met with little success. This was the *Método mui facilissimo para aprender a tañer la guitara a lo Español* (1626) by Luis de Briceño. Briceño had settled in Paris, where he married Anne Gaultier. It is known that he was there as early as 1614, and that his first son was baptized in 1627, with Claude Lesclaut (or Lesclop), an instrument maker, as godfather. Briceño was described as 'maître joueur d'instruments'.[13]

Briceño's book contains simple dance forms and accompaniments for romances, many of them of Spanish origin. In the dedication he reveals the opposition to the guitar:

There are many who ridicule the guitar and its sound. But if they think it over, they will discover that the guitar is the most favourable instrument of our time.

As in Italy, Spanish fashions prevailed, and the guitar had a certain following. However, a number of authorities assert their views of the instrument in no uncertain terms. Mersenne, in his consideration of the four- and five-course guitars,[14] thinks 'its sounds are related to the kettle and it always seems to whine'. Pierre Trichet is more outspoken and soundly berates the followers of Spanish fashion:

The guiterre or guiterne is widely used in France and Italy, still more by the Spaniards, who were the first to bring it into fashion. They know how to use it more foolishly than any other nation, having a particular address in singing and playing their sarabandes, gaillardes, espagnolettes, passemezes, passecailles, pavanes, alemandes and romanesques with a thousand gestures and bodily movements as grotesque and ridiculous as their playing is bizarre and confused. Nevertheless, one finds in France courtesans and ladies who ape the Spaniards, demonstrating that they derive more pleasure from foreign things than those that are natural to them and domestic. They are like those who forsake their own sumptuous fare for the bacon fat (lard), onions and brown bread of others. For who doesn't know that the lute is right for and familiar to the French and that it is the most agreeable of all the instruments of music. Sometimes some of our nation abandon it completely to take up the guitar. Isn't this because it is easier to learn to play than the lute, which requires a long and arduous study before one can acquire the necessary address and disposition? Or is it perhaps because the guitar has some effeminate quality that pleases and charms them and makes them inclined to pleasure? In Ronsard's ode to the instrument:

> Il est des dames pensives
> L'instrument approprié;
> Il est des dames lascives
> Pour les armours dédié.

However, I don't doubt that music can provide other means capable of making playing the guitar more masculine and vigorous, and of giving it some new grace. But it is necessary to await such a happening and to content onself with the daily inventions of musicians of our day who study according to their capacity to discover new things on the guitar to embellish it more.[15]

Expressions of dislike of the guitar occur in later writings in seventeenth-century France,[16] and the lack of sources apart from the works published by the court guitarists would indicate that real enthusiasm was limited to the royal entourage.

The man largely responsible for the favour enjoyed by the guitar in court circles (the fashion was carried to the English court by Charles II) was Francesco Corbetta.[17] One wonders if Trichet would have regarded him as the 'masculine and vigorous' influence had he been writing later in the century. Born in Pavia in or shortly before 1615, Corbetta began his career as a teacher in Italy. In 1639, when his *Scherzi Armonici* appeared, he was teaching in Bologna; *Varii Capricci per la Ghittara Spanuola* was published in 1643 while he was in the service of the Duke of Mantua, and *Varii Scherzi di Sonate per la Chitara Spagnola* came out in Brussels in 1648. These early books reflect a gradual change from the easily acquired strummed style to pieces of a more complex nature.

In 1656 Corbetta was in Paris, where he contributed an interlude to Lully's ballet *La Galanterie du Temps*, in which Louis XIV took part. In 1660 Samuel Pepys accompanied Charles II to England and the monarch's guitar came too. Corbetta followed two years later, and in 1671 the first of his two collections entitled *La Guitarre Royalle* appeared, being dedicated to the King of England. While in England, Corbetta created a following for the guitar and numbered many distinguished people among his pupils, including the future Queen Anne. A work by a Seignio Francisco, *Easie Lessons on the Guittar for young Practitioners; single and some of two Parts*, was recorded in 1677.[18] At this time we know from an entry in a manuscript in the British Museum that Corbetta was employed by the Duke of York:

> *Establishment of wages . . . of the Duke of York, Christmas, 1677: Lady Anne's Guytarr Master, Mr. Francisco Corbet £100 p.a.*[19]

so the work is probably attributable to him.

The often quoted reference to Corbetta in Anthony Hamilton's *Memoirs du Compte de Grammont* is too good a description not to repeat:

> *There was a certain Italian at the court, famous for the guitar. He had a genius for music, being the only one who could do anything with the guitar; but his composition was so graceful and tender that he could have produced*

harmony on the lowest of instruments. The truth is that nothing was more difficult than to play in his style. The liking expressed by the King for his compositions had made this instrument so fashionable that everyone was playing it – well or badly. Even on the dressing tables of all the beauties one could rely on seeing a guitar as well as rouge and beauty spots.

The Duke of York was a passable performer, but Lord Arran rivalled Francisco himself. This Francisco had just composed a sarabande which so charmed or desolated everyone, that all the guitar players in the court set about learning it, and God knows the strumming that ensued everywhere.[20]

In spite of the fact that it was the done thing to play the guitar, not everyone was enamoured of it. Pepys, while admiring Corbetta's ability, was 'mightily troubled that all that pains should have been taken upon so bad an instrument'.[21]

The guitar was not confined to court circles, however. Again we find it surpassing the lute; in 1697 William Turner referred to:

The fine easie Ghittar, whose performance is soon gained, at least after the brushing way, hath at this present time over-topt the nobler lute.

Turner's rider, however, shows that not all guitarists were strummers:

Nor is it to be denied, but that after the pinching way, the Ghittar makes some good work.[22]

Corbetta was not the only influence. Roger North relates that one 'circumstance' that helped 'convert the English Musick intirely over from the French to the Italian taste' was 'the coming over of old Nicholai Matteis'.[23] Later he mentions his 'book which was designed to teach composition, ayre, and to play from a thro-base. And (in it) his examplars were for the Guittare'. This work appeared in 1682 under the title *The false consonances of musick or Instructions for the playing of a true Base upon the Guitarre*, being a translation of an earlier Italian edition. Matteis was a powerful performer; indeed, his guitar was said 'to contend with the harpsichord in concert'.[24] As well as being a skilled guitarist, Matteis was a noted violinist and in the introduction to his work he reveals he knows the lute. The passage allows him to vent his feelings on plagiarism:

> *The Reader is desired to take notice that a certain Lutenist has had ye con-
> fidence to call himself ye Author of this Book when ye truth of it is that I
> presented a Copy of it to a Person of Condition which was Transported by
> myself to the French lute. How this Lutenist came by the Copy of it I know
> not but he has got it & has ye face to entitle himself to ye Composition.*

We have seen earlier the intrusion of the guitar as a continuo instrument in Italy, and no doubt this is where Matteis learned his art. He
finds it necessary, however, to argue the case for basing his work on
the guitar:

> *The Guitarre was never so much in use & credit as it is at this day, &
> finding it improved to so great a Perfection it is my present design to make it
> company for the other Instruments. Every body knows it to be an imperfect
> Instrument & yet finding upon experience how agreeable a part it bears in a
> consort I have composed severall Pieces both for ye practice & enformation
> of those that would make use of it with ye Harpsecord, Lute, Theorbo or
> Bass-Viol.*

A variant spelling, *Kittar*, given by Matteis, provides a link with a
reference quoted by Jeffrey Pulver[25] to four players on the *gittar* in
'the musicians in the Mask 1674'. In the list of materials supplied for
their costumes the spelling is *Gytarrh*, and in the account for these,
Kittar is featured. Another find of Pulver's in the state papers is of
interest here; this is from the Lord Chamberlain's Records for 1686
and is an:

> *Order that the sum of £10 be paid to John Abell, musician in ordinary to
> his Majesty, for a guytar by him bought for his Majesty's service in his bed-
> chamber.*

The guitar faced competition not only from the lute, but from the
cittern also; Thurston Dart comments that John Playford's *Musick's
delight on the Cittern* (1666), the last of the cittern books, 'seems to have
been an attempt to oust the fashionable guitar, introduced by Matteis
and Corbetta a few years earlier'.[26] Playford's views on the guitar are
given in the preface of this work:

> *Not a city dame, though a tapwife, but is anxious to have her daughter
> taught by Monnsieur La Novo Kirkshaivibus on the Gitar which*

instrument is but a new old one, used in the time of Q. Mary as appears by a book printed in English of instructions and lessons for the same about the beginning of Queen Elizabeth's reign, being not much different from the Cithren only was strung with gut strings, this with wyre which was in more esteem (till of late years) than the guittar.

In the following century the fashion was to change to the English guitar, which, in spite of its name, had nothing in common with the guitar. It was more like a cittern in shape and had the tuning: c e g c' e' g'; a similar instrument is the Portuguese *guitarra*, the guitar proper in Portugal being *violão*, a name that preserves the sixteenth-century links with *vihuela* and *viola da mano*. The English guitar flourished in the latter part of the eighteenth century, and no doubt its decline was brought about by the introduction of the six-string guitar. But to return to Corbetta.

His second *Guitarre Royalle*, published in 1674, was dedicated to Louis XIV. It is simpler in style than the first, having been composed (so Corbetta remarks in the introduction) in a style his Majesty would find pleasing. This means that the pieces contain more rasgueado chords than those of the earlier collection. In these books Corbetta abandons the customary alphabet and writes out the chords he employs in letter tablature, thus giving himself more flexibility. The titles of many of the allemandes, sarabandes, gavottes and other forms contain the names of the nobles Corbetta met, some of whom were his pupils – the Duke of York, the Duke of Monmouth and even the King (Plate 31d).

Corbetta visited Spain at some time (in the 1671 *Guitarre Royalle* he mentions his 'return from Spain'). There are a number of references to a Spanish publication by Francisco Corbera, *Guitarra Española, y sus diferencias de sonos*, which, as far as is known, has not survived. However, Gaspar Sanz sang Corbetta's praises in his *Instrucción*; in an appraisal of books by earlier guitarists he includes Corbetta's name with the terse, but revealing remark *el mejor de todos* – 'the best of all'. It is not known if Sanz heard Corbetta play; it would have been possible, but it may be that he was only familiar with his publications.

Corbetta died in Paris in 1681. The guitar, however, continued to survive in the French court in the hands of his pupil Robert de Visée (*c.* 1660–*c.* 1720). The first mention of de Visée is as a theorbo player in 1680.[27] He became a chamber musician at the court, and in 1719 succeeded L. Jourdan de la Salle as the King's guitar tutor, in which post he was followed by his son François in the following year. He published his first work, *Livre de Guittare dédié au Roy*, in 1682. This was followed by the *Livre de pièces pour la Guittare* in 1686. As well as another collection of pieces for theorbo and lute de Visée left a number of works in manuscript.

The contents of the guitar books are suites of various length. His style is more delicate than that of his master; fewer rasgueado chords appear, and a more open texture results. In the preface to his first book de Visée expresses his attempt to:

> *conform to the taste of skilful people, in giving my pieces, as far as my weak talents permit, the flavour* (tour) *of those of the inimitable Monsieur de Lulli.*

A similar style was cultivated by Remy Médard, another of Corbetta's pupils, whose work appeared in *Pièces de Guitarre* (1676) (Plate 33). It is dedicated to Madame la Marquise de Monferer, who was herself a guitarist. Médard tells her he would say she played the guitar well, but this would be to praise himself, as she had chosen him as her tutor. In recommending the guitar 'to all honest people' he gives us some insight into its status and its popularity with the nobility. The 'cavalier and easy character' of the guitar has made it the choice of the greatest Princes of Europe who desire 'gentle amusement'. Nevertheless, its small number of strings and the ease with which one can play some pieces on it have given rise to some abuse of the instrument, but this is the result of ignorance on the part of such performers. Those who take it up, however, will enjoy performing in *spectacles*, *comédies*, and *mascarades*.

Médard claims to have followed the manner of 'the famous Francisque Corbet', imparted to him in the course of several months, with the difference that Médard has found an 'ease' for his pieces that Corbetta did not take the trouble to look for. François Campion (*c.* 1680–1748), carried on the breakaway from the rasgueado style in his *Nouvelles Découvertes sur la Guitare* (1705), notable for its plucked fugal style.[28]

The works of Corbetta and his school can be regarded as the ultimate in development of style of the Baroque guitar. Their compositions fall half-way between the pure rasgueado style that opened the century and lute style; a notable feature of the later books is their concern with ornaments, an obvious lute influence. Changes in tuning were necessary for the realization of their textures. The five-course guitar tunings differed according to the type of music that was to be performed. Scordatura was often practised, but apart from this the changes involved concerned the tuning of the two strings that formed the fourth and fifth courses. According to Gaspar Sanz[29] the tunings customary in Spain were:

these are used for *musica ruidosa* – 'noisy music', that is, music of a chordal texture played rasgueado – and for song accompaniment. The tuning common in Italy was without bourdons:

this was preferred for contrapuntal music, where melodic texture was important. Both Corbetta and de Visée ask for the addition of an octave on the fourth course, which gives the tuning:[30]

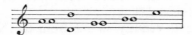

The result is that the fifth course is used as a melody string and so the thumb and forefinger often produce an upper voice in an alternating movement. In this context it should be noted that many modern transcriptions, intended for the six-string instrument, cannot do justice to this repertory.

Present taste has given preference to the contrapuntal style, and the dislike of strummed music has turned performers away from Corbetta. The style has often been dismissed as 'simple'; however, to quote Richard Keith:

> *far from being easy pieces for a plodding or indifferent amateur, the music in the* Guitarres Royalles *is complex and demanding. If the two kings and their followers performed these pieces even passably, they must have devoted*

> *many hours of diligent practice to this impudent little instrument, so sneered at by other musicians of the day and so long confined to oblivion.*[31]

To appreciate the music fully, then, it should be heard on a properly tuned five-course guitar; as yet there is no easy opportunity to do so.

The Spanish Guitar in the Netherlands and Germany

The taste for the seventeenth-century guitar style that had been established in Brussels by Corbetta's visit was carried on by the Flemish guitarist François le Cocq, a musician in the Royal Chapel in Brussels. His book, *Recueil de pièces de guitarre* (1729), contains a preface by its dedicatee, Jean-Baptiste Castillon, Provost of Sainte-Pharaïlde in Gand, in which Corbetta's appearance in the Low Countries and the effect he had are mentioned. After his book appeared, the nobility of Brussels took up the guitar with enthusiasm. At the time of Le Cocq's work the instrument was still in fashion; indeed, the Electress of Bavaria was one of Le Cocq's pupils. Castillon must have been something of a guitarist himself, as he expounds the principles of the instrument and explains the signs found in its tablature. After Le Cocq's compositions he has added a number by composers from the previous century, which include 'N. Derosier, F. Corbet, Gaspar Sanchez, St. Luc, Robert de Visée, de Lelio (probably Lelio Colista, mentioned by Sanz), Perez de Zavala and J. B. Granata'.[32]

Another eighteenth-century source from the Netherlands is the misleadingly named *Princes An's Lute Book*.[33] It is actually a collection of pieces for the five-course guitar, written in French tablature; it includes the first Menuet (Rondeau) from de Visée's Suite No. 9 in D minor. The fly-leaf bears the note:

> *This curious MS was Princes An's lute Book, & presented to Wm. Shield by his friend James Smith.*

Princes An was the wife of William IV of Orange (1711–51). Her book contains 124 pieces arranged in groups according to key; the keys of D, C, G and A dominate the selection. As well as the expected Menuets, Sarabandes, Gigues and Gavottes, it features some unusual titles such as Bobel, Palpie, Aripet and Dority. Many of the pieces are attractive, and although the rasgueado technique appears, it is used sparingly, as the following Menuet shows:

Example 6: Menuet from Princes An's Lute Book

Elsewhere in northern Europe the cultivation of the guitar in no way rivalled its popularity in the south. Its presence in Germany is established by Michael Praetorius, who calls it *quinterna*,[34] a name used a century earlier by Martin Agricola to describe a completely different instrument.[35] Praetorius gives the following account:

> *Quinterna or Chiterna is an instrument with four courses, which is tuned like the oldest first lutes, but is not rounded but quite flat, scarcely two or three fingers deep. Some have five courses, and are used in Italy by Ziarlatini and Salt' in banco (that is, comedians and buffoons) only for strumming accompaniments to Villanelles and other foolish low songs. Nevertheless it can be used to good effect in other graceful Cantiunculae and delightful songs by a good singer.*

It seems Praetorius was well acquainted with the early seventeenth-century Italian strummers.

The simple style reappears in a manuscript collection that was used by Princess Adelaide, wife of the Bavarian Elector, Ferdinand Maria. Her love of music is attested by the fact that she was responsible for the first opera production in Munich.[36] Later in the century Jacob Kremberg's collection of songs *Musikalischen Gemüths-Ergötzung* (1689) appeared. The guitar was added to the lute, the angel lute and the viol to form an accompanying ensemble. In the preface Kremberg advocates octave doubling so that 'the bass does not lose its gravity', and relates that the *Hamburger Cithrinchen* (bell cittern) can be used instead of the guitar if it is strung in a similar manner; he has come across this practice in many places in the Netherlands. Kremberg gives a variety of guitar tunings, the commonest being the usual arrangement of intervals on the five-course guitar.

Solo music for the angel lute appears with pieces for the guitar in a source from the same period as Kremberg's work.[37] The angel lute, an archlute with a number of extra bass strings tuned diatonically, was popular in the second half of the seventeenth century; it was held to be easier than the lute, and was favoured by amateur performers. The guitar pieces in this collection (some have the Italian alphabet with rasgueado strokes, while others are in French tablature) are of unknown authorship, except for a number by Julien Blovin, who is mentioned as being in Rome in 1673.

The Spanish Guitar in Spain

The five-course guitar originated in Spain; it is fitting that the present survey is concluded by a consideration of how the instrument fared there. As in France the most interesting collections of guitar music date from the latter half of the seventeenth century, the first half having been dominated by publications from Italy. We have met one Spaniard whose work appeared early in the century, but outside Spain – Luis de Briceño. Within the country sources are few. One collection, unfortunately undated, in *Música de vihuela* by Antonio de Santa Cruz.[38] In spite of the title and the author's comment that the works it contains are for *biguela hordinaria*, the contents call for a five-course guitar. The chord alphabet is given at the beginning of the book, but this is not used in the tablature, which is in numbers and in the punteado style. The repertory is in the main typical of seventeenth-century Spanish dance forms – Canarios, Marizapalos and others, but four lengthy Fantasias are also included. Interestingly enough, the work is prefaced with advice on *tañer con limpieza*, and these sixteenth-century echoes suggest that the work belongs to the early part of the seventeenth century.

The outstanding man of the guitar in seventeenth-century Spain, however, was Gaspar Sanz. We have found occasion to mention him already for his opinion of Corbetta – 'the best of all'. In view of the extent to which Sanz's works are performed today and the influence they have had, this judgement might well be applied to him.

The details of Sanz's life have proved difficult to biographers. According to Félix de Latassa Sanz was born in Calanda in 1640, educated at the University of Salamanca, where he received the degree of

2 Viola da mano (from an Italian source)

3 Bowed tenor viol

4 Violas da mano (from an Italian source)

1 (previous page) Andrés Segovia

5a & b Violas da mano (from an
Italian source)

5b

6 Angel playing the lute

7 Viola da mano (from an
Italian source)

8

9

8–10 Italian violas da mano

10

11 Spanish vihuelista

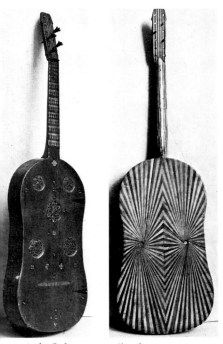

12a & b Sole extant vihuela

13a & b Guitars by Giovanni Smit

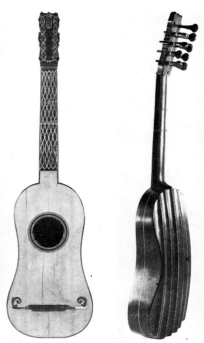

14a & b Guitar by Belchior Dias

15 Early 16th-century five-course guitar

16a Spanish four-course guitarist

LE
PREMIER LIVRE DE
CHANSONS, GAILLARDES, PAVANNES,
Branfles, Almandes, Fantaifies, reduictz en tabulature de Guiterne
par Maiftre Guillaume Morlaye ioueur de Lut.

A PARIS.
De l'Imprimerie de Robert GranIon & Michel Fezandat, au Mont
S. Hylaire, à l'Enfeigne des Grandz Ions.
1552.
Auec priuilege du Roy.

16b Title page of Morlaye's first book of guitar pieces

17a French four-course guitarist

17b Gaspar Duiffoprugcar

18 German four-course guitarist

19 Drawing by Jacques Cellier

20 German bronze casting

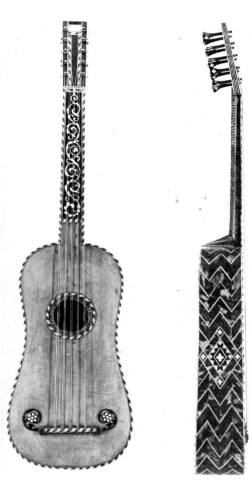

21a, b, c & d Guitar by René Voboam

21d

22a, b, c & d Guitars by Alexandre Voboam and Champion (?)

22b

22d

22c

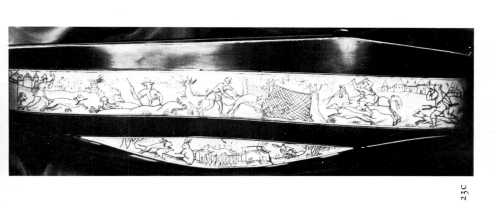

23c

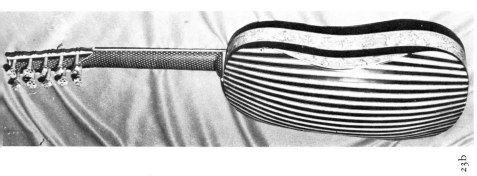

23b

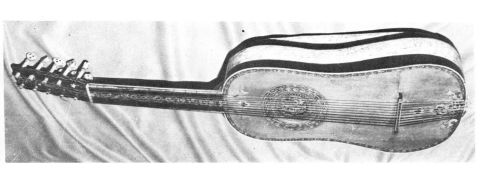

23d Chitarra battente

23a, b & c Chitarra battente by Jacobus Stadler

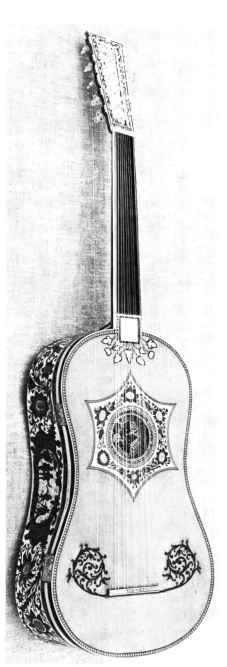

24a–d Six-course guitar by
Joachim Tielke

24b

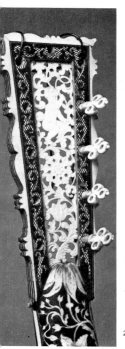

24d

24c

24e Five-course guitar by Tielke

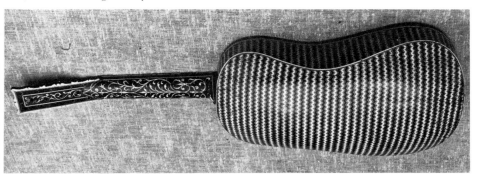

25 Guitar by Matteo Sellas

26a–d Chitarra battente by   26b   26c
Giorgio Sellas

26d   26e & f Guitar (by Sellas?)

27a

27b

27c

27a–c Guitar by Antonio Stradivarius

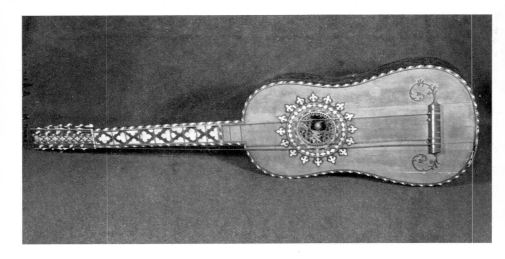

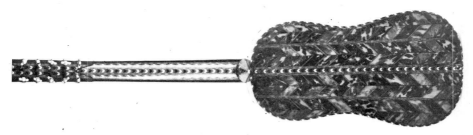

28a & b The so-called Rizzio guitar

28c Guitars in the Royal
College of Music, London

Bachelor of Theology and afterwards became a Professor of Music. Latassa also asserted that Sanz went to Italy, where he studied under Cristoval Carisani, organist in the Royal Chapel in Naples.[39] Rafael Mitjana has questioned his studies with Carisani, as he would have been too young, being born in 1655.[40] A more recent study by Luis García-Abrines casts further doubt on Latassa's account.[41] Sanz's real name, according to the baptismal record, was Francisco Bartolome Sanz, and García-Abrines could find no trace of him as a Professor of Music in the archives of Salamanca University. He suggests that Latassa confused him with another Gaspar Sanz, who studied Theology in the University of Avila and received the degree of Master of Theology in the University of Salamanca. In the light of these difficulties, it will be more profitable to turn to Sanz's work, which gives rise to no confusion.

Instrucción de Música sobre la Guitarra Española first appeared in 1674; in all, eight editions are known, the last being published in 1697. The work is in three parts and it constitutes Sanz's whole output for the guitar. In the Prologue he reveals his intention to publish three more books; the first with many variations on the *sones de Palacio*, the second containing *sonadas, Italianas, caprichos, fantasias, Alemanas, corrientes, gigas* and a great variety of foreign airs, while the last was to be an extended treatment of the art of through bass performance, based on the rules Sanz had learned from his teachers in Rome and Naples.

Sanz was well acquainted with previous publications but complains they are unsuitable for self-instruction. He lists Foscarini (Academico Caliginoso), Kapsberger, Pellegrini, Granata, Lorenzo Fardino and Corbetta. He also wishes to give his Spanish beginners music to play that is familiar to them. In this Sanz signals the lack of native sources in Spain; it is somewhat ironic that performers on the Spanish guitar in Spain had to rely on foreign publications. He refers to Amat's 'little book', which he regards as restricted, and Nicolas Doizi de Velasco is criticized as his tablature is confusing, unlike the Italian alphabet, which is universally used.

The Prologue is followed by a detailed consideration of stringing and tuning the guitar and an explanation of the Italian *Abecedario*. This is given in two Labyrinths, the first of which sets out Sanz's table to enable the performer to play the chord progression of a *Passacalle* in any key and which is similar to the method used by Amat. The second labyrinth is concerned with dissonant chords. To illustrate their use Sanz gives the chord sequences of Spanish, Italian and French dances, signifying their performance by strokes above and below the line. It is interesting to note that he, a Spaniard, advises his readers, if they wish to develop their punteadol skills, to follow the rules of the 'best Maestros of Rome', recommending in particular Lelio Colista, whom Sanz regards as the 'Orpheus of our time'. Colista, who was born in Rome in 1629 and died there in 1680, was a virtuoso performer on the lute, theorbo and guitar. In 1664 he was one of the members of a diplomatic mission to Paris, where it was hoped his playing would make a favourable impression on Louis xiv. The King, a fellow-guitarist, no doubt received him well.[42]

Sanz devotes little space to the alphabet and uses the chord letters only occasionally in some of his pieces. In the main he is more interested in the punteado style, and, in common with the late seventeenth-century French performers, he signifies all the notes individually. Another parallel with the French school is his concern for ornamentation. The abandonment of a heavy chordal movement creates a more open texture that invites the occasional embellishment. Sanz carefully explains the manner of performance of his ornaments, even suggesting the use of trills when they are not indicated, leaving it to the player's discretion. The first part closes with general instructions for figured bass performance on the 'guitar, harp, organ or any other instrument'. Sanz mentions the difficulty of achieving a satisfactory account in the space he devotes to the subject; it really needs a lengthy work, and it will be recalled that this topic was to be the subject of one of his proposed books.

Sanz's music is in vivid contrast to the compositions of the French guitarists. Their style reflects their background, that of the court with all its elegance. Sanz, as he remarks in his Introduction, is more interested in popular forms. He provides a repertory of dances that no doubt enlivened many a festive occasion in seventeenth-century Spain. The music is often lively, most noticeably in the hemiola rhythm of the Canarios, which even permeates the more stately Sarabande. Sanz, however, could also be most expressive in an Españoleta and majestic in a Pavanas, achieving a melodic charm and interest that overshadows the compositions of his followers. The strength of his music has guaranteed it a twentieth-century hearing, and his influence on modern Spanish composers is a testimony to the force of its roots – the music of the people.

Sanz's book was followed by *Luz y norte musical* (1677) by Don

Lucas Ruiz de Ribayez, a work devoted to the guitar and harp. Ribayez is aware of Sanz's compositions, and his own repertory is very much in the same tradition of popular dances. This is also true of the final work to appear in Spain in the seventeenth century, Don Francisco Guerau's *Poema Harmonica* (1694). He was a musician in the Royal Chapel and dedicated his book to Charles II. Though expressly not for beginners it opens with an explanation of rudiments. Of technical interest is Guerau's description of posture, which reveals a concern with punteado performance not found elsewhere. He recommends that the guitar be held stable with the right arm to give the left hand its necessary freedom of movement; the left hand thumb should not protrude from behind the neck as it does on the violin.

The final work to appear in tablature in Spain is Santiago de Murcia's *Resumen de Acompañar la Parte con la Guitarra* (1714). He was tutor to Queen Maria Luisa Gabriela of Savoy, first wife of Philip V. De Murcia's book continues seventeenth-century traditions, being written in numbered tablature based on the chord alphabet. It features the usual *Passacalles* in many keys, but also includes a number of suites, termed *Preludio y Obra*, with such movements as Allemande, Courante, Sarabande and Gigue showing greater foreign influence than the works of his predecessors.

Eighteenth-Century Decline

The dearth of eighteenth-century sources in Spain is similar to the situation elsewhere in Europe. In Austria the sole collection known is one from Aussee (Steiermark).[43] Although Montesardo's chord alphabet is given, the pieces are in French tablature. The collection is notable for an early (the earliest?) appearance of *tremolo* – a group of four semiquavers, the last three of which are repeated notes, higher in pitch than the first. This occurs in the last section of *Schmittcourante*, a variation of the preceding section.

Only isolated sources come from Germany,[44] and it is not surprising to find Jakob August Otto discussing the introduction of the guitar there in 1788 (*see below p. 63*). In France the use of the guitar in providing outdoor entertainment is witnessed by the many paintings of Jean-Antoine Watteau that feature the guitar. A description of such an occasion by Pierre-Michon Bourdelot paints a charming, if somewhat fanciful picture. At open-air performances in the Tuilleries people gather with their lutes, guitars and other instruments. Nightingales and wild birds alight on the necks of the instruments to hear them better, which proves, so the author contends, that birds are more sensitive to the charms of music than to their own liberty.[45]

A mid-century renewal of interest is indicated in the article on the guitar in Diderot and d'Alembert's Encyclopaedia.[46] It had been revived by some amateurs who had awakened a taste for *vaudevilles, pastorales* and *brunettes*, which have benefited from the use of the guitar. Apparently this interest was sufficient to warrant the publication in the following decade of *Les Dons d'Apollon* by Michel Corrette, a method of learning to play the guitar easily from tablature *and* music. The Diderot article gives an account of tablature but makes no mention of the use of normal notation. Corrette (Chapter II) describes the use of the G clef as new, with the sound an octave below the written pitch, which is with us today. Corrette's notation is at a primitive stage; the separate voices are not consistently indicated (Plate 31e). This is also a feature of early notated music for the six-string guitar.[47] Initially violin notation was used, and the development to the standard guitar notation of the nineteenth century took place in Italy, from where it spread to the rest of Europe.[48] It is of interest that Corrette makes no attempt to notate the octave sounds of the lower courses. As his work was published in 1763, the beginning of this practice can be dated *c.* 1760.

The discussion of fingering in Corrette's Method reveals that seventeenth-century compositions were still being played. Indeed de Visée was still popular in nineteenth-century France; transcriptions of some of his pieces were published by Napoleon Coste in his edition of Sor's *Méthode* (*c.* 1845). Corrette's *manière de pincer* still excludes the third finger of the right hand. According to the Encyclopaedia, the right-hand position for plucking was between the rose and the bridge, while the rasgueado strokes, or *batteries*, were performed between the rose and the last fret on the neck (only ten frets were used) (Plate 34); this avoided the hard sound produced near the bridge.

The position of the Baroque guitar is unique in the early history of the instrument; in no other period did it assert its individuality more. In the sixteenth century, the guitar had been overshadowed by the greater lute and vihuela, and the influence of their music is evident in its repertory. In the nineteenth century the guitarist composers also kept close to general musical developments in their compositions. The Baroque guitar, however, falls midway between the two extremes of using the instrument to produce pure art music and as a means of strummed accompaniment. In this combination of rasgueado and punteado it achieved for the first time an identity of its own in the musical world, an identity that, as has been seen, was not to everyone's taste.

Chapter 4

The Development of the Instrument (II): *The Six-string Guitar and the Appearance of the Modern Instrument*

The recent history of the guitar falls into two distinct phases. First, the five-course instrument underwent a number of changes that resulted in the early nineteenth-century six-string guitar; this, in its turn, was modified to become the modern guitar. The most noticeable difference in the later phase is the increase in body size; the most important, however, is the development of fan-strutting or fan-bracing (see below p. 65). This advance in constructional method was by no means universally adopted; it was introduced by Spanish makers, and although some makers in other countries followed their example, the general decline in popularity of the instrument in the second half of the nineteenth century meant that improvements were confined to Spain. Only in the present century has the practice been taken up by makers everywhere.

The Addition of the Sixth String and Constructional Improvements

The use of fan-strutting can be traced back to the closing decades of the eighteenth century. It was in this period also that the changes in stringing came about. As with the addition of the fifth course to the four-course guitar, it is not known exactly when and where the transition to the six-string guitar took place. The rather complex situation does not present a single line of development; there is evidence that in some centres the five-course guitar acquired a further course before the strings became single, while in others it appears that the five-course instrument lost its double strings before the sixth string was added. The extent of the influence of these various instruments on each other has yet to be clearly defined.

First, the six-course guitars. These had appeared during the period of the five-course instrument (e.g. the Tielke six-course guitar), but, to judge from the tuning given by Majer (*see above, p. 22*), they do not appear to have been an extension of the five-course guitar in the sense of an addition of a course a fourth below the standard interval pattern. Six-course guitars with such an extended tuning became established in Spain at some time before 1780; it was in this year that Antonio Ballesteros published his *Obra para guitarra de seis órdenes*. A later treatise for the same instrument, *Principios para tocar la guitarra de seis órdenes* (1799) by Federico Moretti, draws attention to the absence of six-course guitars in Italy and states that 'the French and Italians use single strings on their guitars and hence they can tune more quickly'.[1] Although the guitar with six single strings became the standard instrument in Spain in the early nineteenth century (Aguado published his *Escuela de Guitarra* in Madrid in 1825), the six-course guitar persisted there, and in 1836 an English commentator could write that 'the Spanish guitar is constructed with double strings, which are tuned in unisons, with the exception of the lowest pair, which are in octaves'.[2]

Moretti's observation introduces the second aspect of the problem – the abandonment of courses in favour of single strings. The reason for the change was mainly for musical effect, but practical difficulties played a part. A. Lemoine, in his *Nouvelle Méthode* (Paris, 1790), describes these:

With this method it is rare to play accurately (juste) *and to hear the harmony in all its purity, as* (*the sounds of*) *the two strings* [*of the lower courses, tuned at the octave*] *strike the ear in such a way that the higher sounds are heard before the lower ... Besides ... one can rarely find strings for the unison g's and b's that are of the same size and perfectly true.*[3]

Doisy's *Principes Généraux de la Guittare à cinq et à six cordes et de la Lyre* (Paris, 1801)[4] and an eighteenth-century Italian guitar in the Victoria and Albert Museum, which has a head for five pegs only,[5] suggest that the first step was to a five-string guitar. There do not appear to be any contemporary statements in France and Italy about who was responsible for the change or for the addition of a further string. A German claim was made by the violin and guitar maker Jacob Augustus Otto, which confirms the intermediate stage of a five-string instrument:

The late Duchess Amalia of Weimar having introduced the guitar into Weimar in 1788, I was obliged to make copies of this instrument for

63

> *several of the nobility; and these soon became known in Leipzig, Dresden and Berlin; so great a demand rose for them that, for the space of sixteen years, I had more orders than I could execute.*
>
> *I must here take the opportunity to observe that, originally, the guitar had only five strings. The late Herr Naumann, Kapellmeister at Dresden, ordered the first guitar with the sixth or low E-string, which I at once made for him. Since that time the instrument has always been made with six strings, for which improvement admirers have to thank Herr Naumann.*[6]

Although this establishes the presence of the six-string guitar in Germany, it is unlikely that Naumann was initially responsible for the addition; he had studied the guitar in Italy, and it is more than probable that he had met the six-string instrument there.

Consideration of extant guitars from the eighteenth century that were originally built to take six strings[7] has led to two suggestions as to the area where the instrument first arose: 'along a Paris–Naples axis passing through Marseilles',[8] and 'along an Austro–Italian axis'.[9] Guitars from various centres in France, Italy and Austria date from the 1780s: a guitar by Montron was made in France in 1785;[10] one by Antonio Vinaccia of Naples is also dated 1785,[11] and a guitar by Michael Ignatius Stadlman of Vienna was made in 1787.[12] There is also evidence that the lyre-guitar, which from the beginning had six single strings,[13] played a part in the process of change, if not instigating it, at least accelerating the widespread adoption of the extra string.[14] Thus, on present evidence, all that can be said with certainty is that the guitar with six single strings tuned in the modern interval pattern emerged somewhere outside Spain in either France or Italy.

The musical benefit of a further string that extended the compass downward by a fourth was the avoidance of inverted chords that had plagued the earlier instruments. Thomas Heck comments on the addition:

> *Was this not the minimum improvement necessary to achieve the roots I, IV and V in the lowest three strings (in several keys), while at the same time allowing for triadic, melodic and ornamental use of the upper three strings? The low E completed the double-octave with the first string, e', as well, thereby giving the classic guitar a kind of perfection which the five-course baroque guitar had resisted for about 200 years.*[15]

Two instruments that well represent the transitional period are the six-course guitar by José Benedid[16] (1800) (Plate 34), and the six-string guitar by Giovanni Battista Fabricatore (1798) (Plate 35), both instruments in the collection of Jack and Dorinda Schuman of Cleveland, Ohio. The Benedid table extends into the fingerboard, which has only eleven frets up to the body. The upper and lower bout measurements, 21·5 and 28·7 cm, are only slightly larger than five-course guitar widths; the depth of the body, 9·7 to 10·5 cm, is closer to that of the modern instrument but is not typical of early nineteenth-century guitars. Decoration is limited to simple line inlay in the back and table marquetry below the bridge and in the extension into the fingerboard. The design of the inlay below the bridge is almost identical with the marquetry on a six-course guitar by José Pagés (dated 1798), now in the Victoria and Albert Museum. The Pagés guitar also shares the soundhole surround of two circles of mother-of-pearl diamonds. It has, however, suffered the addition of a modern fingerboard; in its original condition it would have looked very similar to the Benedid guitar.

Although the fingerboard of the Fabricatore guitar extends almost to the soundhole, it is set into the table to lie flush with it (cf. the fingerboard on the guitar by Gennaro Fabricatore, Plate 36c). It is interesting that the higher frets become shorter as they approach the soundhole, as was the fashion when they were set into the table on the five-course guitar; also, there are only ten frets up to the point where the neck joins the body. The heritage from earlier guitars is seen again in the low-bridge position (which allows a string length of 64 cm), the decoration of the bridge ends and the inlaid ivory strips on the neck and heel. This instrument is shallower than the Benedid guitar (it is only 6·5–8 cm), but it is similar in width, although the elongated waist creates a slimmer appearance. The shape of the head complements the body shape and was a favourite design of eighteenth and nineteenth-century makers.

The most important constructional innovation, however, is the appearance of fan-strutting, visible in the Benedid guitar (Plate 35d). The under side of the table carries two struts radiating from the soundhole, and above it there is a star-shaped pattern of struts, presumably meant to render the upper part of the instrument more responsive. The Pagés guitar in the Victoria and Albert Museum collection has a similar strutting pattern; the lower part of its table is supported by four radiating struts, and the star-shaped pattern also appears above the soundhole.

There does not appear to be any literary reference to the introduction of this refinement in table construction, and, to the present writer's knowledge, it appears for the first time in these Spanish-made guitars. The fact that both makers were active in Cadiz and the general similarities between the two instruments suggest that Benedid and Pagés collaborated on problems of construction. Previously the table had been supported by transverse bars only, positioned to withstand the tension of the strings. However, these bars reduce the flexibility of the table, which as a result becomes less effective in transmitting sound. The importance of the fan system of strutting is that, in lying closer to the line of the grain, it frees the table to a much greater extent yet still suppplies the necessary support. This discovery has been of tremendous importance for the guitar and, perhaps more than anything else, it marks its emancipation from the influence of the lute. The phenomenon of fan-strutting is peculiar to the guitar; attempts have been made to improve the lute by giving it a fan-strutted table but without success;[17] it must still rely on the extreme thinness of the table.

In spite of the wide variation in appearance of the five-course guitars of the seventeenth and eighteenth centuries, they shared a number of constructional features. The pegs were of wood. The length of the neck from the nut to the point where it joins the body was only sufficient for at most eleven frets. These were generally of gut; if fixed frets were used, a practice that arose in the eighteenth century, ivory and, later, brass were used. The heel dropped sharply away towards the back (this can be seen in any illustration that shows a rear view of a five-course guitar). The table was generally extremely delicate; measurements of extant instruments confirm the thickness of 2 mm given in a seventeenth-century manuscript.[18] The table extended a little way (4–5 cm) into the fingerboard:

> *presumably as a strength member rather like the deck of a ship, for though the guitar is sonorously one of the most perfect of instruments, it tends to be structurally not the most robust.*[19]

The soundhole was adorned with a carved rose of varied design, often most intricate. The bridge was set low on the table; the distance from the bottom of the body to the bridge was between 7 and

9 cm. This low bridge position made it possible to have a vibrating length of the strings that could vary between *c.* 61–*c.* 65 cm even though the overall length of the instrument was no more than *c.* 89–*c.* 95 cm. The strings were fastened through rectangular openings or holes (Plate 39). The rectangular openings in the bridge on the guitar by Belchior Dias extend down to the table, so that the bridge has a number of feet; presumably this was an attempt to make it more efficient in transmitting vibrations. These bridges gave two possibilities for the height of the strings above the table and fingerboard, depending on whether they were inserted straight through the holes or passed over the bridge first. The body generally showed slight waisting; the range of widths, upper bout 19–21 cm, waist 16–19 cm, lower bout 23–26 cm giving the average proportions 7 : 6 : 8. The backs of the bodies were either rounded or flat; in either case they were often constructed of a number of ribs.

It is significant that some of these features are also found on the lute, and it is understandable that with the decline of the lute in the eighteenth century they no longer appeared on the guitar. The features that disappeared were the curved, ribbed back (flat, two-piece backs were used instead), the carved rose (its disappearance was accompanied by a slight increase in the size of the soundhole) and the low bridge position (raised to the centre of the lower bout); the transition to the nineteenth century was completed by the adoption of a separate fingerboard extending down to the soundhole, the use of machine heads, which made tuning a much simpler business, and the positioning of the twelfth fret over the end of the body. The raising of the bridge did not produce a noticeable difference in string length; a common measurement for this factor is 63–64 cm. A new type of bridge was introduced; on this, the strings passed over a saddle (a strip of ivory that determined the lower vibrating end of the strings more cleanly) and into holes in the bridge and table, where they were wedged by small wooden pegs or pins – hence the name 'pin-bridge'.[20] Finally, changes in the proportions of the body accentuated the waisting; the upper and lower bouts became slightly wider and the waist narrower, sometimes excessively so.

Although the five- and six-course guitars gave way to the six-string instument, they did not completely disappear. The continued existence of the six-course guitar in nineteenth-century Spain has already been mentioned; the five-course guitar has persisted until the present day, at least in Brazil, where it is used by folk musicians. It is known there as the *viola* (the six-string guitar is called *violão*) and it is generally tuned to the pitches of the five upper strings of the guitar. It is interesting that the early practice of doubling at the octave above has been retained; the bottom three courses are so tuned, while the upper two are at unison.[21]

The break with tradition is seen in a guitar by Louis Panormo, which well expresses the instrument's newly found individuality (Plate 38). The label reads 'Louis Panormo, the only Maker of Guitars in the Spanish Style, 46 High Street, Bloomsbury, London: Guitars of every description from 2 to 15 Guineas, 1833'. The instrument is fan strutted, the lower part of the table being supported by seven struts radiating from the cross-bar below the soundhole. Panormo's debt to Spain lies in improvements brought about by the use of fan-strutting, but comparison with a guitar by Josef Pagés, now in the Collection of The Royal College of Music, London, reveals a close similarity in the proportions of the body. The Pagés guitar (Plate 38) carries a label with the information that it was made in Calle de la Almargura, Cadiz in 1809. Its measurements are: overall length 95 cm, string length 63 cm, widths 21–17–27·8 cm, depth 8·9–9·4 cm; the Panormo guitar is slightly wider in the body – overall length 95 cm, string length 63·2 cm, widths 22·5–17·3–29 cm, depth 8·7–9·3 cm. The Pagés guitar has only five fan struts. Another difference is the bridge design; the Panormo guitar has the pins set in a scooped-out rectangle, one of the sides of which acts as a saddle, and exclamation mark ornamentation at each end, while the bridges on the Pagés guitar, probably not original, has a separate saddle. The Panormo instrument retains the sloping heel (Plate 38b), while the design of the Pagés heel (Plate 38d), which is found on other Spanish made instruments of the period, is that preferred by modern makers.

Louis Panormo was the leading maker in England in the first half of the nineteenth century. He was advised on construction by Fernando Sor, who, as a much travelled performer, had a wide experience of makers. Sor reported on the improving standards outside Spain in the *Giulianiad*:

> *The manner of constructing the body of the instrument is almost everywhere understood extremely well, and most Neapolitan, German and French guitars leave, in this respect, very little superiority to the Spanish. In the goodness of the body or box, the Neapolitans in general long surpassed,*

*in my opinion, those of France and Germany; but that is not the case at
present; and if I wanted an instrument, I would procure it from M. Joseph
Martinez, of Malaga, or from M. Lacote, a French maker, the only
person who, besides his talents, has proved to me that he possesses the
quality of not being inflexible to reasoning. The guitars to which I have
always given the preference are those of* Alonzo, *of* Madrid; Pagés *and*
Benediz, *of* Cadiz; Joseph *and* Manuel Martinez *of* Malaga; *or*
Ruda, *successor and scholar of the latter; those of* M. Lacote, *of* Paris;
and M. Shroeder *of* Petersburgh.[22]

The lead taken by Spain is not surprising, considering how domesti-
cated the guitar had become there, as is revealed in an article on the
music of Spain in *The Harmonicon* of 1829:

*The guitar is the instrument most generally employed; it is quite as
national as their beads and their chocolate and is to be found in every house,
from that of peer to the barber.*

In the other countries of Europe makers continued to work along
more or less independent lines, and national characteristics can be
distinguished. The most noticeable feature of northern guitars is that
the waisting is sharper; the upper and lower bouts were widened to
produce a 'double circle' body shape (Plate 37a) while in the South
the shape of 'two joined ovals' was preferred.[23] Further innovations,
which have not stood the test of time, appeared. René François
Lacote, the leading French maker, used rather elegant machine heads
on his later guitars. The gears were concealed inside the wood of the
head and from the front the tuning pegs were not visible; they were
inserted into the rear of the head.[24] Lacote was also responsible for
the use of scalloped fingerboards, referred to and described by
Flamini Duvernay in *A Complete Instruction Book for the Guitar*:

*Some make the fingerboards round like that of a Violin, with sharp frets,
others flat, the frets rounded off. There is also a sort of neck that the Makers
call* Manche coulé, *the surface of which is quite smooth, and the frets,
instead of being sharp and elevated, are made even with the wood and the
interstices slightly hollowed. The last are most preferable, in my opinion,
by reason that the* Glissé *or* Slide *can be effected with much greater strength
and facility.* (Plate 37b.)

In 1822 the German violin and lute maker Georg Staufer was granted a licence to work in collaboration with Johann Ertel on improving the construction of guitars. Two of their improvements were the raising of the fingerboard above the table to create a better tone and the use of an alloy of brass, copper, silver and arsenic – used by button makers in the manufacture of white buttons – instead of silver or ivory for the frets to provide a more durable material.[25]

The situation in England in the first quarter of the nineteenth century is summed up by George Henry Derwort in his *New Method of Learning the Guitar* (1825):

> *As to guitars, the English instrument makers have carried them already to great perfection, and as this instrument is getting now more and more fashionable, the Author is convinced that in a very short time, they will be made here quite as good, if not superior, to the generality imported from abroad.*

However, the 'very short time' did not bring the hoped for improvements in constructional skill. The period in which the above quotation was written was one of prosperity for the guitar in England, but the serious pursuit of the instrument the professional recitalists had inspired did not last. The standards achieved by Panormo were not surpassed; on the contrary, with the rise of the romantic conception of the guitar in the second half of the century instruments such as the one illustrated in Plate 44c were often portrayed in the hands of fashionable young ladies. Even Spain did not escape the decline. A mid-century guitar by Altmira, now in the Victoria and Albert Museum collection, has nothing to commend it as an instrument; it is obviously merely a vehicle for decoration. In spite of the guitar in Plate 41c having been sanctioned by the leading figure of the Victorian guitar world, Madame Sidney Pratten, she did try to maintain standards. A collection of forty-five guitars that had belonged to her and Madame Giulia Pelzer was sold by Sotheby's in 1938. Of these, thirteen were by Panormo, the largest number by any one maker. Several of the guitars described in the Catalogue of the sale are of historical interest; two of the guitars used by Sor are listed, one of which was made by Ramirez of Malaga, and another guitar had been the property of Napoleon – it had been presented to Ferdinand Pelzer, Madame Pratten's father, by his pupil Bacheville, who was one of Napoleon's generals.

Unusual Guitars

The decline of the early nineteenth-century guitar, the representative of the first stage of the development of the modern instrument, indicates that it had failed to win a place among the instruments considered worthy of serious pursuit. This dissatisfaction with the instrument found one outlet in the production of a wide range of variant instruments, their connection with the guitar often only tenuous; indeed, their departure from the basic form of the instrument was sometimes so far that the only link seems to be in the retention of the name 'guitar'. The terminology of these instruments often betrays their origin – harp-guitar, double harp-guitar, harp lute guitar and lyre guitar, although some of these owe their origin to Edward Light and were consequently related to the English guitar with its different tuning and body rather than to the guitar proper.

The appearance of unusual guitars can be traced back, surprisingly enough, to a double guitar made by Alexandre Voboam in 1690 and now in the Kunsthistorisches Museum, Vienna. It consists of two five-course guitars, one of normal size, the other much smaller. The smaller instrument is attached to the larger in Siamese twin style, its bass side joined to the treble side of the 'parent' instrument. This is an isolated instance of a variant instrument in the early history of the guitar. There does not appear to be any reference to the reason for its appearance, and it may simply have been of curiosity value. The theme was taken up again in the nineteenth century; Staufer produced a *Doppelgitarre* of similar construction in 1807. Other makers used the idea of two necks but attached them to the one body.

An extension of this principle appeared in J. F. Salomon's Harpolyre, which incorporated three necks set into one body, shaped like the lower half of the normal guitar. An account of this instrument in *The Harmonicon* of December, 1829 reveals the philosophy behind its introduction:

> *Many distinguished professors of the guitar have endeavoured to raise the instrument from the inferior rank which it holds in the sonorous class. But vainly has their skill conquered the difficulties of fingering &c; still only a thin, brief and dry sound has proceeded from the frail machine; and while the talent of the performer is admired, we regret to see the talent wasted in conquering the defects of an unfavourable instrument.*

Various efforts were made to ameliorate the construction of the guitar, but without success. Its primitive form was changed for that of the ancient lyre about twenty-five years ago; yet the alteration was productive of no advantage as regards the sound, which indeed, was rendered less intense. It was necessary to revert to the old construction, with one additional chord.

Mr. Salomon's improvements on the primitive guitar are not of this slight character. The instrument is wholly reconstructed in his Harpolyre, without being materially increased in size, while its volume of sound is augmented in a tenfold degree, and its resources for execution out of all comparison with what they formerly were. The following details will render this evident:

The harpolyre is provided with twenty-one strings divided on three necks. The central, or common, neck has six strings like the ordinary guitar and arranged in the same manner; that is mi, la, ré, sol, si, mi. The only difference consists in the greater number of stops on that of the harpolyre. All ordinary guitar music may be executed on this neck, with the advantage of a stronger sound and more harmonious effect. The left neck (looking at the instrument in front) is called the chromatic, and is furnished with seven strings in silk, covered with silver twist. The right neck, to which Mr. Salomon has given the name of the diatonic, is furnished with eight strings of gut.

The power of this instrument, its sonorousness, its capabilities of varying are such, that it is scarcely possible to describe bounds to the effects which may be derived from it. For example, there are two distinct qualities of sound in the harpolyre. The central neck produces sounds full and voluminous, and the diatonic gives about those of the ordinary guitar. From the combination of these sounds, the most singular and delightful effects may be anticipated. Messrs Sor and Carcassi, who have examined this novel instrument, are both sensible of its advantages, and engaged in composing music for it. With a little study, any person who plays the guitar may learn to use the two additional necks.

Despite this favourable reception, the harpolyre, which was described as 'a new guitar', did not become established.

The reference to 'the ancient lyre' in the above quotation introduces a class of variants where again only the lower half of the guitar body was used – the lyre guitar. Instruments of this form had appeared during the Middle Ages and the Renaissance, and they enjoyed a new vogue in the last quarter of the eighteenth century and the first two decades of the nineteenth, one of the results of renewed interest in Classical Antiquity.[26] The lyre guitars had only one neck, but each side of the sound box extended upwards into two curved arms, which were sometimes joined to the neck at the top to resemble the ancient Greek lyre. Other unusual guitars also dispensed with the upper half of the guitar body. On the *Wappengitarre* (shield guitar), which appeared in Vienna at the beginning of the nineteenth century, the upper bout ended in two pointed extensions or was simply squared off. The harp-guitar made by J. Beckhaus of Philadelphia, now in the Crosby Brown Collection in the Metropolitan Museum of Art, New York, had the normal guitar neck with the half body extended downwards in a pillar with its own soundhole. In the playing position this pillar served to support the instrument on the floor. One can regard these instruments as attempts to put into practice the principle that, as the upper part of the guitar body adds little to the production of sound, it might just as well be omitted.

A shield guitar constructed by the French maker Vissenaire in 1825 had a number of extra bass strings which left the bridge at an angle and were attached to an extension of the head. Several makers used this idea to extend the range of the normal guitar to create a class of instruments known as bass guitars. The extra strings were tuned diatonically and played open; because of this they generally lay off the fingerboard, but sometimes, as on the bass guitar by Lacote in the Stearns Collection in the University of Michigan, the fingerboard was widened to cover all the strings, but the frets served only the higher, stopped-down strings. Such guitars were usually intended for accompaniment, but the use of an eleven-string guitar by a certain Spanish concert artist was reported at the end of the century.[27] The fingerboard was wide enough for seven strings and the instrument was tuned:

In the present century Narciso Yepes has reintroduced a similarly extended guitar. The instrument he favours has ten strings and a very wide neck as all the strings lie over it. The extra strings have been added for two reasons; first, as an attempt to strengthen weak responses on the six-string guitar, and second, to accommodate early lute music more easily and more faithfully than is possible with only six strings. As yet this ten-string guitar has not gained a wide following.

In the nineteenth century the extension of the guitar by the addition of further strings in the bass had its counterpart in guitars where the strings appeared in the treble. An early example of this is a guitar, now in the Victoria and Albert Museum, made by Rafael Vallejo of Granada at the end of the eighteenth century (Plate 40). To the six courses on the normal neck are added ten courses ingeniously arranged on the treble side of the instrument. The short playable area of the neck would allow chords to be produced to accompany a melody on the higher pitched strings. The words 'I belong to King Charles IV' are inscribed in Spanish on the belly.

An instrument featured in the Great Exhibition of 1851 enjoys the best of both worlds by being extended in both the treble and the bass (Plate 41). It was invented by Don José Gallegos of Malaga and is described in the Catalogue of the Exhibition:

> *The tone of this ingenious piece of mechanism comprises that of the harp, guitar and violincello; it has thirty-five strings, twenty-six of which and twenty-one pegs act upon the harp, producing in their full extent the diatonic and chromatic scales: six strings belong to the part of the Spanish guitar, while the violincello part has three silver strings and eighteen pegs. The pedestal by which it is supported is so constructed that the instrument may be either elevated or depressed at pleasure.*

The Catalogue, perhaps fortunately, does not give any details of how the instrument, known as a *Guitarpa*, was to be played.[28] A similar supporting stand, but for the guitar, had appeared earlier in the century. This was the *tripodion*, the invention of the guitarist Dionisio Aguado. His rationale for this device included freeing the player from the task of supporting the instrument and, in thus removing the guitar from contact with the body, the production of greater volume. He also lists the advantage of being able to perform on the higher frets, which previously had not been used; presumably he meant the frets above the twelfth. Aguado specifically mentions that with the tripodion it is no longer necessary to support the right hand by resting the little finger on the table. The 'machine', as it was sometimes called, was used by Sor, whose *Elegiac Fantasia* was composed to be performed with the aid of the tripodion; Aguado quotes from the preface to this work:

I should never have presumed to impose on the guitar a task so onerous as that of producing the effects required by the nature of this piece, but for the excellent invention of Mr. Aguado . . . . without this invention, I should not have imagined that the guitar was capable of rendering, at the same time, the different qualities of tone requisite to the part which contains the melody, to the bass, and to the harmonic complement, or part containing the accompaniment.[29]

The unusual guitars considered above departed from the basic form of the instrument to a greater or lesser extent. There existed also in the nineteenth century a range of guitars that differed from the ordinary guitar only in their size. This was determined by the pitch of the strings, which, however, retained the interval pattern of the standard tuning. In this category come the *Terz* guitar, the *Quarte* guitar and the *Quinte-Basse* guitar; the first was tuned a minor third higher, the second a fourth higher than the pitch of the normal instrument, while the last was a fifth below. There was even an *Octavine*, a small guitar tuned an octave above standard. An early reference to such an instrument occurs in General T. Perronet Thompson's *Instructions to my Daughter for Playing on the Enharmonic Guitar* (1829), but it is not clear from the context that they were being made. The octave guitar in Plate 44, in the collection of Jack and Dorinda Schuman, suggests that it was not common, at least in England, until later in the century. The instrument bears a label that reads: *The Bambina No. 8; Introduced by Mrs. Sidney Pratten, London, 1871.* The string length of this rather charming little guitar is 33·5 cm. Of this group of instruments only the Terz guitar seems to have met with any degree of success; a considerable body of music exists for it, and Giuliani even composed a Concerto for it and arranged works for Terz guitar and string quartet.

General Thompson's *Instructions* is not a tutor in the sense of being concerned with technique and the practical business of playing the guitar but a short treatise attacking equal temperament in general and on the guitar in particular. The application to the guitar of the tuning system he advocates resulted in a most unusual pattern of zig-zag frets (Plate 42); in all other respects the instrument remained unaltered. General Thompson (1783–1869) was a Fellow of Queens' College, Cambridge from 1804 to 1814; the title-page of the *Instructions* anonymously describes the Author as 'A Member of the University of Cambridge'. His book, the outcome of five years devoted to the problems involved, arose out of 'a desire to abate the untuneableness of the Common Guitar'. This had resulted in the situation that:

> *no professional singer would think of being accompanied on the Guitar; and if the instrument maintains its ground in practice at all, it is in consequence of its convenience, of fashion, and, above all, of the badness of people's ears.*

General Thompson's solution was to apply the 'Enharmonic principle' to the placing of the frets; that is, instead of the octave being divided into twelve equal parts, as in equal temperament, a division of fifty-three parts is used, which is termed 'the approximative scale'. The positions of the intervals of just intonation are found along this scale, and the corresponding position of the frets to give the intervals for one key on the guitar are worked out. This process is repeated for all the other keys and the resulting positions are noted. To cover all the possibilities it is necessary to divide the fingerboard (up to the twelfth fret) into fifty-nine parts; the lines drawn across the fingerboard are called 'bars'. Each bar has twelve holes, arranged in six pairs to accommodate one fret for each string. The frets are shaped like croquet hoops and are wide enough to serve one string only.

The fingerboard is then fretted for a chosen key; the head of the guitar carries a small plaque with the words 'Key of   ', where its name can be entered (in the illustration the guitar is fretted for the key of A). The majority of the frets are 'of a blue temper'; it is recommended that 150 will be adequate, which makes provision for losses. These are used for all the notes except when these occur on adjacent bars; in this case brass frets are inserted in the position nearer the bridge. There are twenty of these, and they are filed down so that the string does not catch them when it is depressed on the fret above. When one changes key, further fret positions are required, as some of the notes of the new key do not correspond to those of the old. The newcomers are signified by white frets (we are told twenty will suffice). However, it is not necessary to add frets for all the different notes of the new key; only those that are needed in the music should be provided for.

In view of the complexity involved in arranging the Enharmonic guitar and the practical difficulties of performance, it is hard to imagine that it became popular, particularly among young ladies, for whom, as the Author informed his brother-in-law in a letter,[30] the *Instructions* was written. Although the Enharmonic guitar was advertised as made and sold by Louis Panormo, there do not appear to be any that have survived. The *Instructions* is a very learned work and it provoked a lively correspondence in *The Harmonicon*. *The Westminster Review* for April 1832 carried a long and favourable review in an equally learned style. which is not to be wondered at as General Thompson had become half-owner and editor of the periodical and wrote the favourable notice himself.[31]

These unusual guitars played no part in the main lines of development that were to lead to the modern instrument and, after enjoying a brief vogue, they were forgotten. The feeling of dissatisfaction with the early nineteenth-century guitar, which had given rise to so many of them, was also felt in Spain, but here the approach to the problem concentrated on refining the advances made at the end of the eighteenth century – the employment of fan-strutting. Towards the end of the nineteenth century at least one author commented on the superiority of guitars made in Spain.[32] The man responsible for this happy situation was Antonio de Torres Jurado (1817–92), and the fine guitars he produced have been a lasting source of inspiration to his successors.

The Modern Instrument: Torres and After

Torres was taught the principles of guitar making by José Pernas,[33] but soon surpassed his master (Plate 43). His most important contribution was the extension of the fan-strutting system, but he also established the vibrating length of the strings at a constant 65 cm. and increased the size of the body. Since the time of Torres it has also become standard practice to make the fingerboard at least 5 cm. wide at the nut. The fingerboards of early nineteenth-century guitars were quite narrow, as were those of five-course guitars, in spite of the double strings, which might seem to guarantee adequate width. Too narrow a fingerboard limits the freedom of movement of the left hand fingers, necessary in the performance of contrapuntal music. The increase in size of the six-string guitar was thus a slow process; the instrument had acquired its sixth string in the second half of the eighteenth century and it was not until the second half of the nineteenth century that larger guitars appeared. The earlier development in size of the five-course guitar was similarly tardy; the sixteenth century five-course guitars were as small as the four-course instruments, and it was not until the seventeenth century that the larger instrument became standard.

Torres was the first of a distinguished line of Spanish makers; Vicente Arias (*c.* 1845–1912), Manuel Ramirez (1869–1920), Enrique García (1868–1922), Santos Hernandez (1873–1951), Domingo Esteso (1882–1937), Francisco Simplicio (1874–1932) and Marcelo Barbero (*d.* 1957), all of whom produced instruments of the first rank. Their guitars present a similarity in appearance, revealing that at last a uniformity of approach to construction has been established. The woods used in the best instruments are fine-grain spruce for the table, which is sometimes stained to complement the dark rosewood of the back and sides, cedar for the neck and head and ebony for the fingerboard. Decoration is limited to a mosaic inlay surrounding the soundhole, made up of coloured pieces of wood arranged in a pattern to the maker's design (Plate 45). Sometimes the same inlay is echoed in the bridge decoration, but generally the maker rests content with a simple ivory purfling; this also serves to protect the wood from the pressure of the strings. The overall effect is one of great beauty with the splendour of the wood enhanced by simple lines and elegance of form.

Particular differences discernible in modern guitars reflect the individual contribution of the maker. Sometimes this is merely a question of design, as for example in the shape of the head, which often becomes the maker's trade mark, but in other cases the differences reveal his approach to the problem of achieving the best possible sound. Variations in the dimensions of the body and string length, the thicknesses of the woods and the fan-strutting pattern are evidence of the luthier's own ideas on the subject. Torres demonstrated the importance of fan-strutting by constructing a guitar with papier maché back and sides and still producing an instrument with a remarkable tone. This does not mean that the wood of the back and sides is unimportant; but by isolating the table Torres highlighted the importance of this part of the instrument.

It is in the strutting of the table that modern makers have experimented most. The Torres system consists of seven struts radiating from below the soundhole with two further struts placed at the outer edge of the 'fan' and tangentially to the lower curve of the table. This pattern can be regarded as the standard system, but the experiments of modern makers have resulted in arrangements that at times depart radically from it. The number of struts used can vary; as few as three have been used with great success. Some makers invert the shape of the fan so that the struts radiate from the bottom of the table, while others place the struts to lie parallel to the line of the grain of the table. One of the most recent developments has been the extension of struts from the lower part of the table into the upper bout, a feature of guitars by the French maker Robert Bouchet and some of the instruments from the workshops of José Ramirez.

These improvements brought about greater volume and helped create a balanced tonal response. A further advance came with the introduction of nylon and its adoption in the manufacture of strings in 1946.[34] Up till then gut strings had been used, but their tendency to break, particularly the top string, and their uneven response made them unsatisfactory. Nylon brought a new dimension of sound; the rather muffled tone of gut strings gave way to a clarity of voice that, though brilliant, did not lack warmth.

The view expressed by Gerald Hayes that 'the guitar has suffered a process of coarsening during the past 150 years'[35] cannot be allowed to stand without comment. It is based on a preference for the sound of the five-course guitar because this was closer to that of the lute. The historical facts are that the five-course guitar was rejected by performers in favour of the early nineteenth-century guitar; this also was felt not to be adequate, and makers, very often in close consultation with performers, initiated further developments. The result has been an instrument very different from the early guitar; the present writer prefers to regard this development as a process of refinement in achieving an instrument of noble tone and with a wide range of expression.

The difficulties inherent in the form of the guitar make successful construction a most demanding task. The maker's abilities as a craftsman in wood are taken for granted; it is possible for anyone with such talents to produce an instrument that *looks* splendid but which disappoints in its quality of sound. The outstanding maker must also be able to select wood, particularly for the table, that will respond well in the final product. In the course of construction small adjustments are necessary to ensure the best result possible with the woods in hand, one of the main tasks being the achievement of a balanced response throughout the whole range. The skilled luthier's approach is far removed from the techniques of mass production, and although his constant aim is high sound quality, it must be appreciated that this is in terms of each instrument. The maker cannot guarantee that his next guitar will sound just like the previous one.

The traditions of guitar construction so firmly established in Spain during the last hundred years have been maintained there by a number of modern makers. Hernandez y Aguado and Manuel Contreras in Madrid, Ignacio Fleta in Barcelona and others continue to uphold the high standards of their predecessors, while some Spanish makers have carried their craft to other countries, particularly America. The methods employed by Spanish makers are somewhat different from those generally followed elsewhere, and it is only rarely that a non-Spanish maker has produced instruments that compare with theirs. One such maker was Hermann Hauser (1882–1952), whose guitars have been played by some of the leading recitalists. The present century has seen interest in construction spread as far as Japan, and no doubt more makers of distinction will emerge outside Spain. David Rubio (Plate 47) is the first English guitar maker to achieve international recognition. After gaining experience in Spain and the United States, he returned to England and is now established in Duns Tew near Oxford. As well as guitars he makes lutes, vihuelas and other early plucked instruments and has recently had a further workshop built specifically for the construction of harpsichords. Rubio has collaborated with Julian Bream and speaks highly of his insight into the construction of guitars. Such contact with a virtuoso performer who also appreciates instruments from a technical point of view is most beneficial. At present José Romanillos from Madrid is established in the workshops that adjoin Bream's home in Dorset. He has produced guitars of various sizes in his constant search for his ideal sound.[36]

The present discussion has been in terms of guitars of the highest quality. These are naturally very expensive and are suitable only for the recitalist or the very advanced amateur who can do justice to their potential. One of the strengths of the guitar, however, is that it is possible to produce instruments of modest price yet suitable for the performance of classical music. This is an important consideration as the beginner can easily acquire his own instrument. The present revival of interest in lute playing has been restrained by the prohibitive cost of the instrument.

The development of the guitar from the small four-course instrument was a complex process that spanned four centuries. The transformation to the modern instrument was a gradual one, with the increases in the number of strings and in the overall size of the instrument taking place only at long intervals (Plate 45). However, there existed in the sixteenth century an instrument with the same tuning as the modern guitar and of a similar size; Bermudo reported that such an instrument was used in Italy.[37] One naturally wonders how the history of the guitar might have been affected had this instrument become established. The extra range afforded by the six courses might have resulted in this vihuela achieving a status similar to that of the lute and the vihuela with lute tuning and consequently inspiring a literature to compare with theirs, which the early guitar was unable to do. Unfortunately, this was not to be – or, perhaps, fortunately, as the rejection of this vihuela with guitar tuning allowed the guitar to develop at its slower pace and eventually to achieve permanent acceptance in our own day. The result of this has been that it is now in the process of inspiring the music it deserves instead of having to rest content with a repertory from the past.

Chapter 5

Classical and Romantic:
The Nineteenth Century

The Early Nineteenth Century Guitar in Europe

After the calm of the eighteenth century Europe witnessed an intense renewal of interest in the guitar, the result of the appearance of the six-string instrument. From the many practitioners who played, composed for and taught the early nineteenth-century guitar two stand out – Fernando Sor and Mauro Giuliani. They both surprised and delighted the audiences of many countries with their music and left in their wake an enthusiastic following to champion the new instrument. Their compositions are still often performed, and their studies, particularly Sor's, are most beneficial in the development of technique.

The revival of interest in Spain began with the work of Father Basilio, a monk of the Citeaux order, whose real name was Miguel García. He was organist at the convent in Madrid, but turned to the guitar, reviving the punteado approach and raising the instrument from its role of strummed accompaniment. His fame grew to such an extent that Charles IV invited him to perform at the Escorial, where he remained in service to Queen Marie-Louise as guitar tutor, including many illustrious people among his pupils. His influence was felt by Don Federico Moretti, who extended Basilio's style and published his own method in 1799. In the same year there appeared another method by one of Father Basilio's pupils: Fernando Ferrandière's *Arte de tocar la Guitarra española por música*. These men were important in laying the foundations of the nineteenth-century revival, but it was Fernando Sor and his lesser known compatriot, Dionisio Aguado (1784–1849), who were to complete the work and carry it to the rest of Europe; they both expressed their indebtedness to Moretti for introducing them to the possibility of part-writing for the guitar.[1]

Sor was born in Barcelona on 13 February 1778.[2] His father, Juan, was a talented amateur guitarist, and Fernando inherited his liking for the instrument; in view of the lack of sources relating to the single string guitar in Spain in this period, it seems likely that it was the six-course instrument that Sor first studied. It was intended that Sor should be trained for a military or administrative career, but his father's death in 1790 put an end to the plans made for him. However, he was fortunate enough to continue his education at the monastery in Montserrat, and it was here that he acquired a solid foundation of harmony, counterpoint and composition. Sor left the monastery when he was seventeen years old and returned to Barcelona, where he recommenced the study of the guitar; it was at this time that he came under the influence of Moretti's compositions. Sor was also greatly impressed by the Italian opera company performing there, and this inspired the composition of his first opera *Telémaco en la Isla de Calipso*, which was presented on 25 August 1797. It was a success, and Sor found himself a celebrity.

Shortly afterwards Sor went to Madrid, where music flourished at the court of Charles IV. Here he came under the patronage of the Duchess of Alba, whose *salon* vied with that of the Benavente-Osuna family. The latter supported Luigi Boccherini (1743–1805), who became involved with the guitar as the Marquis of Benavente was an enthusiastic amateur performer. The instrument is featured in twelve of Boccherini's quintets and one of his symphonies.[3] In spite of the composer's dislike of Spanish folk music, the fourth guitar quintet includes a Fandango; this originally appeared in Op. 40, No. 2, the manuscript of which bears the note 'Quintet imitating the fandango played by Padre Basilio on the guitar'. The symphony, which is scored for guitar, two principal violins, two violins *ripieni*, viola, 'cello, double-bass, two oboes, two French horns and bassoon, is really a chamber ensemble in *concertante* style. The manuscript of the symphony includes a sketch showing Boccherini's preferred arrangement of the instruments in performance; the guitar is placed in the front rank between the first principal violin and the double-bass.[4]

The death of the Duchess of Alba in 1802 left Sor without support. However, he was fortunate to come under the protection of the Duke of Medina-Celi. For several years Sor enjoyed considerable freedom, being entrusted with light administrative duties only, and among his compositions from this period are two symphonies, three string quartets and a number of songs. But political events then disturbed the even pattern of his life. Unrest within the country gave Napoleon an opportunity to interfere; forcing the King to abdicate, he installed his brother Joseph on the throne. There is some doubt about Sor's position; some reports make him sympathetic to the French, while other accounts see him simply as a victim of circumstances. Whatever the nature of his involvement, when Spain gained her independence once more, Sor felt his wisest course was to leave the country. He crossed the border to France in 1813, and it was from this time that he dropped the *s* from his baptismal name of *Sors*.[5]

Sor made for Paris where he was to remain for two years. The first publications of his guitar music date from this period, when he probably became established as a teacher of the instrument. An unsuccessful application for a vacant post in the Royal Music Chapel may have induced him to move to London, where he gave a number of successful guitar recitals. Theatre productions also occupied his attention, and it was for the production of his ballet *Cendrillon* that he returned to Paris. The success of the ballet provided Sor with funds for travel, and his career as a recitalist continued in Moscow. The fame he achieved as a performer was augmented by the production of two of his ballets there, *Alphonse et Leonore* (1824, first produced in London in 1820) and *Cendrillon*, and Sor was invited to St. Petersburg to play before the court. The patronage promised by the Empress Elizabeth did not materialize, as she died shortly afterwards. However, Sor was commissioned to write a funeral march on the death of Alexander I; this led to a further commission, his ballet *Hercule et Omphale*, regarded as his most important work.

In 1823 Sor had married Virginie Hullin, the *première danseuse* of the Paris Opera ballet troupe. She accompanied Sor to Moscow and was so well received that she remained as a teacher when he returned to Paris. Her remarriage in 1838 indicates that she must have obtained a divorce from Sor.

Sor's return to Paris was marked by an unsuccessful production of his ballet *Le Sicilien ou l'amour peintre*. After a short trip to London, Sor returned to Paris, where he remained until his death in 1839. This final period is notable for his association with Aguado. He and Sor were great friends in spite of their different approaches to the guitar, and Sor dedicated his duo *The Two Friends* (Op. 41) to him. Aguado returned to Spain in 1838, the year before Sor's death. In his last years Sor played in public and taught, one of his pupils being Napoleon Coste (1806–83), whose promising career was brought to an end when he broke his right arm in an accident. There is no doubt that Sor's death – from cancer of the tongue – was hastened by the untimely death of his only daughter Julia in 1838. She was an attractive and talented girl, and, according to a report of the final months of his life, her loss rendered Sor almost insane with grief.

The other leading virtuoso of the early nineteenth century was Mauro Giuliani. There has been much confusion over Giuliani's dates, but it has recently been established that he was born in Bisceglie in Italy on 27 July 1781.[6] Little is known of Giuliani's early life, and it is not until he arrived in Vienna in 1806 that his career can be followed. Here his playing soon brought him fame, and many favourable reports of his performances appeared in the German press. In 1808 he played before an audience that included Beethoven, and in 1813 and 1814 he was one of the musical celebrities who formed an orchestra for performances of Beethoven's music. Giuliani may have played the 'cello, as Isnardi states he was trained on this instrument. Giuliani appeared with the pianist Hummel and the violinist Mayseder in a series of concerts named the *Dukaten Concerte*, as the subscription price for the six concerts was one ducat. These were given in 1815; a similar series of three concerts was held in 1818, when Giuliani played with Mayseder and the pianist Moscheles. So successful were they that a further concert was arranged for charity, the beneficiaries being the Needlewomen's Society. In the summer of the same year the trio participated in an *al fresco* concert arranged in honour of the Archduchess of Parma, the former Empress Marie-Louise, on the occasion of her name-day.

In 1819 Giuliani left Vienna in unpleasant circumstances; certain charges had been brought against him, and the police seized his household goods. He travelled to Venice, where he wrote to his publisher, Domenico Artaria, to tell him of his plans. These included a tour of the Continent – to Paris, and returning to Vienna via the Low Countries and Germany. However, the projected trip was not to be, and Giuliani made his way to Rome, where opportunities for recitals were greater than in the North. It was in Rome that Giuliani's daughter, Emilia (*b.* 1813), was educated at the convent *L'Adorazione di Gesù* from 1821 to 1826. Towards the end of 1823, perhaps for health reasons, Giuliani travelled south to Naples, where in the November of that year he gave a recital on the lyre-guitar, and in 1826 he played before Francis I. Two years later he was joined in a concert by Emilia, who was already a proficient performer on the guitar. But by this time Giuliani's health appears to have been failing.

He was not present at a solo recital by Emilia, and his death was reported on 14 May 1829 in the *Giornale delle Due Sicilie*:

> *On the morning of the eighth of this month Mauro Giuliani, the famous guitarist, died in this capital. The guitar was transformed in his hands into an instrument similar to the harp, sweetly soothing men's hearts. He is succeeded by a daughter of tender age, who shows herself to be the inheritor of his uncommon ability – a circumstance which can alone assuage the sadness of his loss.*[7]

The importance of Vienna as a musical centre in the eighteenth and nineteenth centuries is well known. It seems natural that the guitar should have found a home there, and in fact Vienna had a tradition of guitar playing before Giuliani settled there. The atmosphere was propitious to chamber music, and the guitar was often featured in domestic music making. Against this background a number of minor figures flourished; however,

> *It would not be possible, on the basis of the knowledge we currently possess, to argue that there existed a Viennese 'school' of guitarists of which Giuliani was the leading exponent. There was, however, a great deal of activity on the classic guitar in Vienna, which resulted in a minor deluge of printed music for this instrument. Most of the works by Call, Molitor, Klingenbrunner, Tandler, Töpfer, Graeffer, Schulz, Diabelli, Fier, Mendl Wolf, and others of basically German background unfortunately do not equal the compositions of Giuliani as far as style, wit, and suitability to the guitar are concerned. The former should be regarded as evidence of the earliest rise of the classic guitar to cultural (if not artistic) significance in the Imperial City.*[8]

Many Italian names figure in nineteenth-century guitar history, but they found little encouragement to stay in their own country; Vienna, Paris and London were more profitable for them. Matteo Carcassi (1792–1853) from Florence and Ferdinando Carulli (1770–1841) from Naples were two such artists, the former touring extensively, the latter pursuing a more settled career in Paris. Carcassi, too, finally made Paris his home, where he to some extent stole his compatriot's thunder. Perhaps the most familiar Italian name to be associated with the guitar, however, is that of Nicolo Paganini, who, as a background to feats on the violin, cultivated the guitar, which he studied when for health reasons he was forced to lay aside the violin.[9] His compositions that involve the instrument, Op. 39 to Op. 77,[10] include works for solo guitar, violin and guitar duets, trios and quartets. These, however, do not reach the complexity one might expect from the man whose performances on the violin were the talk of Europe. The guitar is used in an unextended way, largely in a chordal accompanying role. He is often quoted as saying of the guitar 'I love it for its harmony; it is my constant companion in all my travels', but he appears to have turned against the instrument in his later years.[11] While in Paris, Paganini was lent a guitar made by Grobert of Mirecourt, an important centre for instrument makers. He signed the instrument before returning it, and it was later presented to Hector Berlioz, who added his signature before donating it to the collection of instruments in the Conservatoire de Musique.

Berlioz was extremely fond of the guitar. He includes it in his *Treatise on Modern Instrumentation and Orchestration*, but treats it in a rather limited way. He perhaps realizes this as he comments:

> *It is almost impossible to write well for the guitar without being a player on the instrument. The majority of composers who employ it are, however, far from knowing its powers; and therefore they frequently give it things to play of excessive difficulty, little sonority, and small effect.*[12]

He advises would-be composers to turn to the compositions of 'such celebrated guitarists as Zanni de Ferranti, Huerta, Sor &c.', if they wish to see what can be done with the instrument. Berlioz also provides some insight into yet a further decline the guitar was to suffer after the excitement of the early decades of the century:

> *Since the introduction of the pianoforte into all houses where the least taste for music exists, the guitar has been little used, save in Spain and Italy. Some performers have studied it, and still study it, as a solo instrument, in such a way as to derive from it effects no less original than delightful. Composers employ it but little, either in the church, theatre or concert room. Its feeble sonority, which does not allow its union with other instruments, or with many voices possessed even of ordinary brilliancy, is doubtless the cause of this. Nevertheless, its melancholy and dreamy character might more frequently be made available; it has a real charm of its own, and there would be no impossibility in so writing for it as to make this manifest.*[13]

The limited technical possibilities expounded by Belioz are mirrored in the works of composers who were not themselves primarily guitarists. The unextended use of the instrument by Boccherini and Schubert[14] is to some extent explained by the fact that they were not writing for the virtuoso performers, who provided their own music. Consequently their guitar parts, like many in the nineteenth-century (Giuliani's are a notable exception), would have been performed by amateurs, and the basic essential of such compositions is that they should be playable with little effort.

Another factor to be considered is the dearth of theoretical information. The only treatise that dealt theoretically with the guitar, as opposed to the many practical tutors, appears to have been *L'Harmonie appliquée à la Guitare* by Carulli.[15] However, it was written for amateurs, to enable them 'to extract and compose accompaniments for the guitar without the aid of a Master', and Carulli specifically mentions that it is 'not at all a complete treatise of Harmony or Composition'. He deals with chords and their inversions, and although non-harmonic notes are mentioned, Carulli decides that the guitar offers only two satisfactory means of accompaniment – chords and arpeggios. Thus the advice given by Berlioz was necessary to anyone wishing to write for the guitar; unfortunately no composer of standing chose to follow it, and it is to the music composed by the guitarists themselves that one must turn to discover what was possible on the recently extended instrument.

The early six-string guitar gave rise to an extremely large quantity of music, which ranged from elementary pieces to large-scale concert works. In spite of the multitude of practitioners, or perhaps because of them, many of the works betray a rather tedious sameness. Of the easier works there are some that can still charm, but on the whole the writing is cliché-ridden. The more extended works also vary in quality. Sometimes it is merely a question of producing a vehicle for technical display with fast scale passages and impressive sounding arpeggios, when the listener may marvel but not be moved. On the other hand Giuliani could produce a sparkling concerto, with virtuosity the handmaiden of real expression. As is to be expected of a new instrument, a great part of the literature is devoted to the cultivation of technique, and the fact that much of this material, particularly the studies of Sor, Carcassi, Coste and Aguado, has adapted well to serve the development of modern technique is indication enough of its value.

29 Four-course guitarist playing from tablature

30a & b Spanish vihuela tablatures

30d Spanish four-course guitar tablature

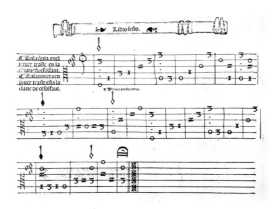

30b

30c Italian four-course guitar tablature

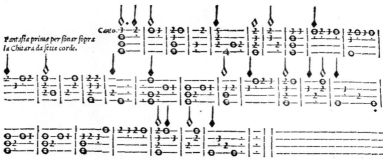

30e French four-course guitar tablature

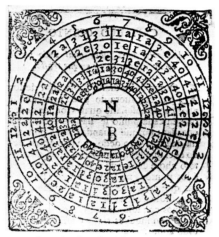

31a Amat's chord table

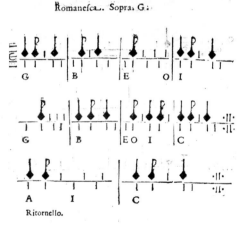

31b Italian chord symbols
with rhythm signs

31d Late 17th-century French
tablature

31c Mixed tablature

31e The beginning of modern guitar
notation

32 Francisco Corbetta

33 Title page of Médard's
Pièces de Guitarre

34 Sketches of a guitarist
by Watteau

35a–e Six-course guitar by Benedid

37b

37a & b Guitar by Weissberger

36c

36b

36a

36a & b Six-string guitar by Giovanni Battista Fabricatore
36c Fingerboard of guitar by Gennaro Fabricatore

38a

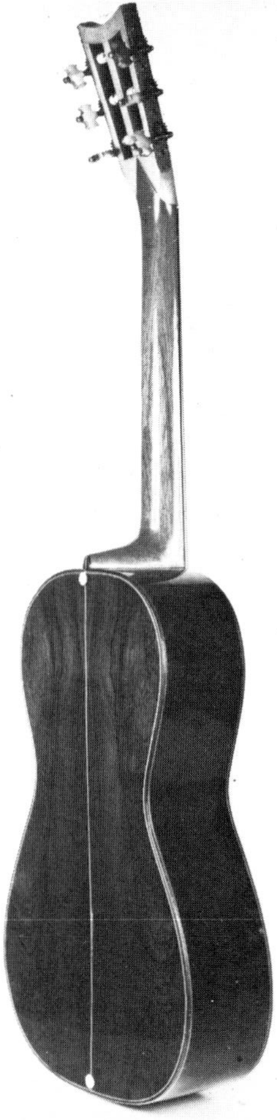

38a & b Guitar by Louis Panormo; 38c & d guitar by Josef Pagés

38b

38c

38d

39a–e Types of bridges

39a

39b

39c

39d

39e

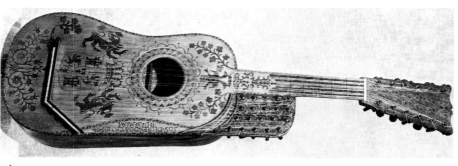

40a

40b

41

40 & 41 Unusual 19th-century guitars

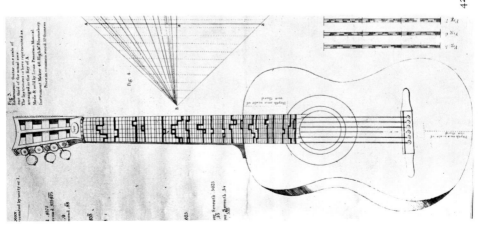

42 The Enharmonic Guitar; 43a Guitar by José Pernas; 43b a Torres guitar

44d (above left) The Bambina guitar; 44a Madame Sidney Pratten

44c Ornate late 19th-century guitar

44b 19th-century hand positions

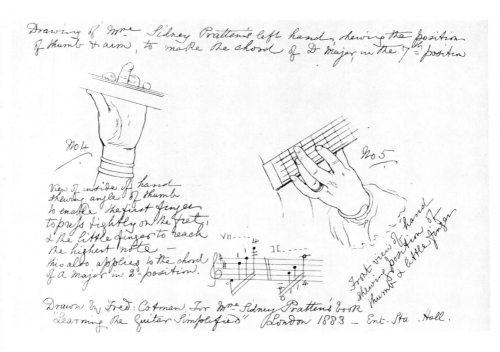

45a The physical growth of the guitar

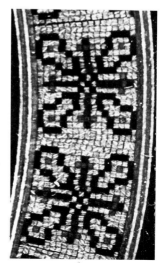

45b & c Modern decoration
45c

46a   46c   46b

46d

46a–d Early 19th-century guitarists

46e Miguel Llobet

47 David Rubio

46f John Williams and Julian Bream

The compositions of Sor and Giuliani set a standard not matched by the other guitarist composers of their day, and they were more successful in creating a repertory of works that find a place in the programmes of modern recitalists. At the other end of the scale they produced works that pleased, and still please, the amateur performer. Their style owes more to Haydn and Mozart than to any nationalistic expression, which may explain why their compositions found universal acceptance. William S. Newman has commented on Sor:

> *The creative worth of Sor's guitar sonatas is high. The ideas, which grow out of the instrument yet stand up well enough apart from it, are fresh and distinctive. The harmony is skilful and surprisingly varied, with bold key changes and with rich modulations in the development sections. The texture is naturally of interest too, with the melody shifted from top to bottom, to middle, and frequent contrapuntal bits added. Among the extended forms, the first allegro movements still show considerable flexibility in the application of 'sonata form', especially in the larger number of ideas introduced and recalled. For that matter, the style still goes back to that of Haydn and Boccherini, especially in the first movement of Op. 22, which has all the neatness of syntax and accompaniment to be found in a classic symphony, and its third and fourth movements, which could nicely pass as a Minuet and Rondo by Haydn.*[16]

Sor's introduction of new material in what is normally the development section of the sonata has been accounted for by William Sasser as a consequence of the limited resources of the instrument, which naturally determine what can be achieved in the composition of extended forms.[17] Both the lute and the guitar are restricted in the number of voices that can be maintained, and this results in 'a pseudo contrapuntal style (*Freistimmigkeit*) in which there is no strict adherence to a given number of parts, that is, in which voices are allowed freely to enter or drop out, and in which also chordal elements occur'.[18] Sasser draws a useful distinction between 'part' and 'voice' in relation to guitar music; he defines 'voice' as 'any single sound or note indicated in the vertical plane of the score', while 'a part may consist of from one to three voices (rarely four), depending on the function of the part in the musical texture.' He regards Sor's works as *freistimmig* strictly in relation to the number of voices, and less so with regard to the number of parts (Sor generally maintains three).[19] Within the restrictions Sor still manages to be engaging, largely through his fertile melodic invention:

G

Example 7: from Sonata Op. 25, First Movement, Allegro non troppo

Giuliani's sonata output was limited to one – Op. 15. His most important compositions are the Concertos, Op. 30, Op. 36 and Op. 70, the last for Terz guitar; only the first of these has received a modern hearing. His forte as far as the solo instrument is concerned is the Theme and Variations, a popular form in Vienna[20] and also with many of the other guitarist composers of the nineteenth century. Giuliani's skill in weaving a melody into a texture idiomatic to the instrument is a constant feature of his art, and it is evident in the short introduction and statement of the theme from *Grand Variations on the French Air 'Partant pour la Syrie'*; (the original song, here transposed from D major for comparison, is taken from Alfred Bennett's *Instructions for the Spanish Guitar*):[21]

Example 8: (a) Partant pour la Syrie, (b) Giuliani's Op. 104, Introduction and Theme

Giuliani also composed works for the guitar and other instruments;[22] the guitar appears with string quartet (Op. 65, and arrangements for Terz guitar, Opp. 101, 102 and 103), violin and 'cello (Op. 19), and violin or flute (Opp. 84 and 85). In his writing for these combinations Giuliani achieved a satisfactory balance, always a problem where the guitar is concerned.

Although Sor and Giuliani cannot claim a position of the first rank in the history of music, there is no doubt that they made a distinguished contribution to the literature of their chosen instrument. This, however, was insufficient to guarantee the continuity of interest in the guitar, and, before further developments gave it a new lease of life, the instrument was to suffer yet a further decline. This is well illustrated in its history in nineteenth-century England.

The Early Nineteenth Century Guitar in England

The effect of the early nineteenth-century virtuosi can be gleaned from the music journals of the period. Fétis reported many appearances of guitarists in *La Revue Musicale*, the German press contained similar eulogies and in London *The Harmonicon* provides an interesting record of how the guitar fared in England. An account of its arrival is given in *The Giulianiad*,[23] one of the first periodicals to be devoted to the guitar, which appeared in 1833:

> *The successful introduction of the guitar into England has been comparatively of recent date. Till the peace of 1815, it may be assumed that few persons in this country were acquainted with its full and varied powers. From that time, however, to the present moment, no instrument can be brought in comparison with its rapid advancement in public estimation. No instrument in fifteen years has attained such decided success and extensive circulation. This may in a very great degree be ascribed to the many excellent masters with which the Continent has furnished us; to them must we concede the merit of having given the guitar a character which antecedently was unknown in England, and of having brought it to its present high state of fashionable popularity. But although these masters have effected much, a great deal more remains to be done. Giuliani, Carulli, Sor and other distinguished masters are yet, at best, but imperfectly understood.*[24]

The critics writing in *The Harmonicon* view the recently favoured instrument with less enthusiasm:

March 1824

Review of 40 Easy Pieces and Short Preludes by Carulli;
Amongst the once-favoured musical instruments, now for some time neg-
lected, and coming into practice again, is the guitar. To the exquisite and
wonderful performances of M. Sor this may be attributed; he makes the
instrument 'speak so sweetly and so well' that hundreds fly to 'strike the
chorded shell', who never before dreamt of what it was capable of producing.
Its powers in almost every hand but his are certainly very limited, and even
he, the modern Jubal, cannot give it strength enough of tone to render it
useful anywhere but in a small room. As an instrument, however, for the
boudoir – or still better for the alcove – it is poetical and romantic, and will
always possess charms, both in itself and from association.

M. Carulli's elementary book is a very good and useful work; the airs, if
not strikingly new and melodious, are pleasing and shew good taste. The
fingering is good, and the preludes, which do not attempt too much, prove, so
far as they go, that the author is well acquainted with harmony and is master
of some of its effects.

March 1827

1. A Course of Preceptive Lessons for the Spanish Guitar designed for the
assistance of Master and Pupil: by James Taylor. Two Books.
(Lindsay, 35, High Holborn, Clementi & Co., and Cramer & Co.)

2. Three Waltzes for ditto: A. T. Huerta (Mori and Lavenu, 28, New
Bond St.)

The author of the Preceptive Lessons says 'the experience of 30 years has
convinced me of the difficulty of procuring guitar music sufficiently easy and
progressive for beginners; this, added to a desire to save myself the trouble of
writing lessons for my scholars, has induced me to publish this work, which is,
in fact, little more than a printed copy of those exercises &c. which, in the
course of teaching, I have been in the habit of supplying to my pupils in
manuscript'. He afterwards adds, what we are much pleased to find con-
fessed by a master of this instrument, that 'the guitar is less used as a solo
instrument than as an accompaniment to the voice, and as the principal
object of all the pupils I have taught has only been to play a few light airs,
with occasional variations, and above all to accompany the voice in
singing *– for such are these preceptive lessons intended'. This shows the*
author's good sense; the guitar thus employed is, in a private room, very
delightful: but to introduce it in a grand public saloon, for the purpose of

93

tinkling on it a concerto or sonata is, in our mind, the height of absurdity. Mr. Taylor's instructions are clearly delivered, his examples are well-chosen, and the accompaniments show him to be an experienced musician.

The three waltzes by Signor Huerta are the first of his productions that we have seen. They are not, we conceive, what he means to rest his fame on, but rather fugitive trifles, intended to answer a temporary purpose. We therefore shall not examine them minutely, but merely hint that an attention to the rules of harmony is indispensable in guitar music, which is in the constant employment of chords, simultaneously struck or in arpeggios, and the present publication either abounds in errors of the engraver, or its author has suffered many things to escape him which stand in great need of correction.

February 1829
Review of Giuliani's 3 Rondos for 2 guitars; revised and fingered by Derwort (Paine and Hopkins)
Duets for guitars! – what a feast for those who delectate in congregated nasal twangs! But seriously, this instrument, so romantic and charming in its natural vocation, is little better than a mockery when florid compositions, such as most of these, are given to it. The guitar is for the bower, of the boudoir, and to accompany tender tales of love. It is not amiss as a companion to the dessert to assist the voice in a romance, or in an unpretending arietta. But give to it brilliant compositions, requiring the execution of a violinist, and suited, so far as manner is concerned, to the concert room, it then becomes as ineffective as a piping bull-finch perched on a trombone in the midst of a military band.

June 1831
from Diary of a Dilettante;
ANOTHER PRODIGY: An infant Paganini on the Guitar
An evening paper states that a musical phenomenon has just arrived in London – a first-rate guitar player, although only eight years of age. 'His name is Jules Regondi. The Figaro, *the* Journal des Débats, *the* Journal de Paris, *and* Galignani's Messenger *speak of him with rapture. They say that, in addition to the mechanical precision, which generally is not to be acquired on the guitar under twenty years' practice, he evinces taste and feeling rarely witnessed in a performance on that instrument!'*

Mercy on us! twenty years in learning to play on the guitar! For heaven's sake let the instrument be hereafter put into the hands of none except those of the Struldbrugs, the immortal inhabitants of Luggnagg, who must needs have a vast deal of spare time at command. The French Journals, too, speak of Jules Regondi with rapture, and, doubtless, we shall all soon be elevated to the 'third Heaven', as saith Mr. Gardiner, by this miraculous child, who, in spite of his tender years, has discovered the means of applyng high pressure to music, and reduced the labour of twenty years to the space of about four For we cannot suppose that he commenced his operation still well on his legs; unless, indeed, he began while yet unborn – a thing not impossible to those who believe the story of the holy babe who sang a hymn, to his mother's great surprise, before his entrance to the world.

Dilettante's jocular tone is somewhat modified, however, after hearing Regondi play:

August 1831

Among the musical wonders of the day is Giulio Regondi, the child whose performances on the Spanish guitar are not only calculated to surprise but to please even connoisseurs. This most interesting prodigy, for such he may be termed, who has only reached his eighth year, was born at Lyons; his mother being a native of Germany, but his father is an Italian. To say that he plays with accuracy and neatness what is difficult is only doing him scant justice; to correctness in both time and tune he adds a power of expression and a depth of feeling which would be admired in an adult; in him they show a precocity at once amazing and alarming; for how commonly are such geniuses cut off by the preternatural action of the mind, or mentally exhausted at an age when the intellects of ordinary persons are beginning to arrive at their full strength.

The personal appearance of the almost infant Giulio at once excites a strong feeling in his favour. A well-proportioned, remarkably fair child, with an animated countenance, whose long flaxen locks curl gracefully over his neck and shoulders, and whose every attitude and action seems elegant by nature, not art, immediately interests the beholder; but when he touches the strings, and draws from it tones that for beauty have hardly ever been exceeded – when his eye shows what his heart feels, it is then that our admiration is at the highest, and we confess the power of youthful genius.

The criticisms voiced in some of these extracts are to some extent realized by the writers in *The Giulianiad*, who, as might be expected, take pains to champion their instrument. A short essay *On the capabilities of the Guitar* assesses the instrument's potential from the point of view of harmony, melody and execution. To show the harmonic possibilities, the example is put forward of:

> *M. Czerny, the celebrated piano-forte player, who, in his great admiration of one of Giuliani's concertos (the third), has actually written the whole piece for the piano-forte.*[25]

Giuliani's harmonies were preserved, although the greater resources of the piano were made use of. On the topic of melody, the author grants superiority to 'all sustained instruments', by which he means wind and bowed instruments, but he insists that 'in comparison to the piano-forte or harp in this respect, the advantage must, most assuredly, be given to the guitar', and, in support of this, he goes on to say: 'Those who have heard Giuliani touch this instrument will not hesitate one moment in confirming this'. The guitar's 'powers of execution' are praised 'because we see in the instrument greater perfection in the higher qualities of tone, harmony and expression' rather than 'in the velocity by which it can express certain passages'.

The instrument's main claim to fame, however, seems to be its charm as an accompaniment to the voice. This aspect is taken up in a later article, and the enthusiasm expressed accounts for the very large number of songs published with guitar accompaniment. The essay *On the comparative merits of the piano-forte and guitar naturally* comes down in favour of the guitar:

> *The piano-forte, from its powers, is certainly calculated for exhibiting in the drawing-room the full and instrumental accompaniments of modern composers and dramatic performances; but then it must overpower and drown the slender voices to which we have alluded, as the works of Rossini, Pacini, Bellini and other noisy composers, will sufficiently testify. But for the plaintive ballad, the heroic verse of romance, or for any simple melody portraying some of the finest feelings of poesy, the all-subduing tones of the guitar are unquestionably the fittest.*[26]

The final point is more telling:

> *It is equally agreeable in the hands of either sex; there is nothing exclusive in the use of it, being fitted for all. It lends a charm to the graceful appearance of the one sex, and realises the romantic ideas of the other.*[27]

Naturally much space is devoted to Giuliani. The eulogy accorded him mentions his superb tone production and powers of expression supported by a well-controlled technique. The guitarist is urged to emulate him and 'sacrifice execution to tone, and tone to expression'.

Sor is not forgotten, if only through a letter from an anonymous 'N', who gives an account of his first appearance in London:

It is a fact that until the arrival of Sor in this country, which took place about fifteen or sixteen years ago, the guitar was scarcely known here, and the impression he then made on his first performance at the Argyll Rooms, which I attended, was of a nature which will never be erased from my memory; it was at once magical and surprising; nobody could credit that such effects could be produced on the guitar*! indeed, there was a sort of suppressed laughter when he first came forth before the audience, which, however, soon changed into the most unbounded admiration when he began to display his talents. London was, at that time, not without persons who* professed *to teach the guitar; and I know that several of the guitar-quacks went there 'to* scoff, *but remained to pray'.*[28]

The disadvantage of the small voice of the guitar is recognized in a later article *On Public Performance on the Guitar*:

People hearing a performance on the guitar in a large room, for the first time, are generally disappointed. The reason is obvious: not taking into consideration the limited powers of the instrument, so far as loudness is concerned, they misdirect their attention from the merits of the instrument, and fix it on its want of power, which is its greatest defect. The merits of the guitar to the ear are like those of a miniature to the eye; they both court the most searching scrutiny and minutest examination. Heard or held afar off, where the nicest delicacy of shade and tint are not discoverable, they both lose their greatest charm.[29]

A criticism is offered of performers who try to force the volume:

Playing generally in a large room, they naturally wish that every part of the audience should hear, and in doing this they wholly mistake the manner in which it can be successfully effected. They pull the strings with so much force, for the purpose of producing a loud *tone, that, although they produce more noise, they in fact lessen the real tone of the instrument. Their want of knowledge in acoustics is here verified. It is not the* largeness *of tone that travels furthest and quickest, it is the* quality *of it. A mere whisper, if the tone be sweet and compact, will find its way to every corner of a large theatre, while an overstrained string will produce a tone which will fall, so to speak, dead and lifeless.*[30]

An interesting footnote here refers to Paganini's tone on the violin, described as 'by no means large, but earnest, intense and searching'. The theme of the guitar's lack of volume is taken up again in an introduction to reviews of public concerts. The author thinks a large concert room is not suitable for the guitar and, in suggesting ideal settings, he reveals the true nature of the majority of the guitar's following:

At this season of the year, when the buds and blossoms of flowers are breaking, or have already broken, into freshness and beauty, what instrument can discourse so blandly and bewitchingly in the embosomed and fragrant arbour?[31]

Other settings include:

On occasions of boating, while sailing in calm tranquillity on the silvery bosom of some quiet or rippling lake, whilst the moon may lend its mild rays to the scene, – at such a moment, what so sweet and touching as the music from this instrument? In a gipsy party also – where there must be a sprinkling of romance, and an oblivion of the dull cares of the world – where, we say, there must be these, or the very appellation of gipsying would be a fraud on the intention – what instrument can be listened to with so much reverence and buoyant pleasure?[32]

The picture that emerges is one of extremes. The virtuosi performed to general acclaim, but in the main their music was too difficult for all but the most dedicated amateur. The demand was for easy music – the publishers constantly asked the Sors and Giulianis to supply this – and many were content to supply a rather monotonous accompaniment to a song. No doubt this came about as a result of the guitar finding adherents at every level of society. Madame Sidney Pratten taught Royalty, Sor found a patron in the Duke of Sussex and both music and tutors were dedicated to members of the aristocracy. The guitar even appeared in the kitchen:

We have frequently heard many curious anecdotes of servant girls giving themselves airs *when they went to engage themselves; but the following may be relied on as a fact. A lady who kept a seminary in Somers Town was in want of a housemaid; she advertised, and many called to offer their services. The lady was pleased with the appearance of one, and entered into an agreement with her, requesting her to come to her place without delay. The girl seemed as if she had something on her mind; and, after a grand effort, she said that she would like to go out twice a week for the first month. 'Oh! (said the lady) you attend some particular chapel, I conclude?' – 'No, Ma'am, (simpered the girl) but I am learning the guitar and have paid for a quarter's instruction in advance, so I should not like to lose my lessons.' – 'Where do you intend to practice?' (sic) said the lady. – 'In the kitchen, I suppose,' answered Sappho Cobwebbo. – 'Oh! I shall grow distracted, (said the lady) what with the young ladies thumping upstairs and you thrumming below; – you won't suit me. Good day to you.'*[33]

To cater for such a wide range of needs and abilities a variety of tutors appeared.

Tutors and Technique

At the simplest level George T. May's *Instructions for the Spanish Guitar* (? 1830) (Plate 46) presents a series of arpeggios followed by a few short pieces; it concludes with a number of songs to guitar accompaniment which form the greater part of the work. A more ambitious approach is to be found in Marziano Bruni's *Treatise on the Guitar* (1834); in the Preface he expresses a reaction against the use of the guitar in a facile way:

Having acquired, both here and abroad, some reputation as a Professor of the guitar, the Author trusts that his experience of the capabilities of this interesting and fashionable instrument particularly qualifies him for facilitating its acquirement, not merely to the limited extent of an accompaniment to the voice. but to the more ample range of an effective performance of grand and brilliant Concertos, Fantasias &c.

There are many brilliant passages upon the guitar which have generally been considered of such extreme difficulty as to deter pupils from even attempting their execution. These passages, for which the professors who alone have hitherto succeeded in conquering them obtain immense applause, are like the egg of Columbus, difficult only to those who are unacquainted with their mechanism, but extremely easy and simple when this is known. In the present work, the Author has applied himself particularly to explaining these apparently miraculous effects, and has given examples of every possible combination upon the instrument, all of which he has rendered capable of being executed by any learner of moderate capacity. Such are the claims which he humbly puts forth to the patronage of amateurs of the guitar, and he leaves it to a discerning Public to judge whether these claims be well or ill-founded.

Similar high aims were expressed by Ferdinand Pelzer in his *Instructions for the Spanish Guitar* (?1830):

In writing instructions for the Guitar it has been usual with many masters to teach it according to their own style of playing; or, in other words, in that style which their own continual practice had rendered most easy to themselves. This, as in painting, produces a Mannerism which cannot fail to become tiresome. My object and intention are, after leading the beginner by the most simple and easy progress to a knowledge of the fingerboard of the instrument, to teach him every position of the fingers of the left hand, and every mode of striking the strings with those of the right, which can be required in the execution of any compositions for the guitar, whether by Carulli, Giuliani, Sor, Aguado, Nüske or any other Master. By thus combining all the different modes of fingering, that distinction between them, which ought never to have existed, will be done away with, and the pupil will acquire a more thorough knowledge of the instrument and a greater facility in executing whatever music may be set before him.

Noble sentiments, but in a later work, Pelzer himself gives way to popular taste. In the introduction to the first issue of his *Guitarist's Companion* he writes:

The object of The Guitarist's Companion *is to put into the hands of the Amateur such music as is strictly appropriate to the Guitar, – songs and other pieces so assimilated with its character that they could not be performed with more becoming effect on any other instrument whatever; and that the work, when complete in Twelve Numbers, should form an acceptable* Travelling Library *to the Guitarist and Singer.*

The standards established by the leading recitalists were to some extent continued by Pelzer's daughter, Catharina Josepha, later to become Madame Sidney Pratten after her marriage in 1854 to Robert Sidney Pratten, a noted flautist. In her youth she gained fame as a performer on the Continent and in London, beginning at the age of seven. She played with Giulio Regondi, and in the thirties was London's fashionable guitarist. In 1836, when she was only fifteen, a critic commented:

> *She played three brilliant pieces, accompanied by her father, to the general admiration of the company assembled. Her touch is powerful and her execution wonderful; we were surprised how such tiny fingers could draw forth such perfect sounds from an instrument requiring some strength to make it discourse.*[34]

Madame Pratten's own didactic publications also reflect the changing standards of the nineteenth century. Her most ambitious work was a *Guitar Tutor*, which contains numerous exercises for both hands that range over the complete fingerboard and which includes works by Sor and Giuliani. However:

> *Madame Pratten found, when she commenced teaching the guitar, that the amateur pupil was not inclined to devote sufficient study to the instrument to gain the necessary technique to grapple with the difficulties of the music of the classic authors for the guitar. The works of Giuliani and Sor, Legnani, Nüske and Schulz were beyond the powers of the average student.*[35]

As a consequence of this sorry state of affairs, *Learning the Guitar Simplified by Mme. Sidney Pratten* appeared. Described 'as used by Her Royal Highness the Princess Louise and Her Royal Highness the Princess Beatrice', it was a popular work as it ran to at least ten editions. To the exercises and scales in each key is added a 'Pleasing Piece or Song', and to make things as easy as possible a diagram of the fingerboard appears on every other page to facilitate the location of the notes. A further publication designed to familiarize the player with the fingerboard was *Colored (sic) Diagrams of the Notes of the Fingerboard of the Guitar* (1891), in which each note of the diatonic scale was assigned a different colour. Another popular tutor, *Instructions for the Guitar tuned in E Major*, was aimed at 'those who have little time for practice, or take up the Instrument late in life' to enable them 'to learn more elegant effects and numbers of pieces or songs in a shorter space of time than in the ordinary key'. However, works of some difficulty appeared for the E major guitar, for example D. J. M. Ciebra's *Fantasia*,[36] a theme and variations, which, according to the title page, 'was played by himself at the Queen's Concert Rooms, Hanover Square'.

The advice given on various aspects of technique varied from tutor to tutor. There was no standard method of holding the instrument:

> *As to the manner of holding the guitar, every nation differs in it. The Italians hold it otherwise than the Spaniards; the French ladies make a violincello of it; the Germans hold it in an oblique position, neither quite horizontal nor perpendicular.*[37]

Sometimes the instrument was supported on the left leg resting on a foot-stool,[38] but the right was also used; Sor held the instrument in this way (*Method*, 1830) and it was advocated by Flamini Duvernay, who, according to the title page of *A Complete Instruction Book for the Guitar*, was 'Guitarist to the King's Theatre':

> *The right foot should be placed on a small Ottoman or anything else that will elevate the right knee above the other, then place the guitar horizontally above the knee, slightly inclined backwards towards the chest, on which it should repose, the head of the neck a little elevated, so as to facilitate the change of positions.*[39] (Plate 46d)

A common recommendation was the use of a ribbon, which was necessary, as was Aguado's tripodion, to hold the guitar steady. The significance of this general lack of stability in the position of the instrument is that much nineteenth-century guitar music and, of course, the simple song accompaniments do not leave the first position (that is, with the first finger at the first fret). It is only when more ambitious music is performed that the instrument must have more support to enable the left hand to move freely to the higher positions.

The positions of the right hand described in the tutors also reveal no general agreement. The practice of supporting the hand by placing the little finger on the table persisted and is repeated in the majority of tutors. This approach is recommended as late as 1881:

> *Place the little finger on the sounding-board about two inches above the bridge. Place the thumb on the large silver E string, raise the wrist about two inches and a half so as to enable the three fingers to fall easily on the*

three Gut strings, then place the first finger on the G string, the second on the B string and the third finger on the E string.[40] (Plate 44a and b)

However, Nicario Jauralde warns that:

The little finger is never used in playing, but is left free without leaning on the guitar; whereas, if it were placed otherwise, it would not only impede the movement of the hand in the changes of Piano and Forte, but would prevent the other fingers from acting with agility.[41]

Good advice on the action of the fingers was given by Duvernay:

And to bring forth a good and pure tone, the thumb must be quite outside the fingers, so as not to impede their movement when striking a chord.[42]

Generally the use of the thumb and the first two fingers of the right hand was preferred; Aguado is positively against the use of the third finger:

To make the most of the guitar, I strongly recommend the use of the middle finger of the right hand, rather than of the third or ring-finger, which is much weaker. It is very essential that the fingers which twitch the strings should be strong.[43]

In producing sounds, the fingers played *tirando*, to use a modern term – the tips rise after plucking the strings. It is not certain when the modern technique of *apoyando* – the finger pushes through the string and comes to rest on the string below – was first employed for the fingers. It was definitely used for sounds produced by the thumb:

The manner of producing the best tone with the thumb is to strike across and to stop on the next string, so that the hand finds a support, and you will obtain all the sound the instrument is capable of without altering the vibration.[44]

If apoyando was used for the fingers, it does not appear to have been discussed at any length. The following brief comment by Alfred Bennet suggests that the technique was not unknown:

In striking the strings, the fingers should press them downwards, and not pull them upwards, as on this depends the beauty of the tone.[45]

Indirect evidence comes from the music. In his Op. 111, Parte II, No. 3[46] Giuliani inserts the direction *Marcate le note di sopra*, and the best method of emphasizing the single notes of the upper melodic line would be to play them apoyando. However, this important aspect of technique was not to become generally established until a much later date.[47]

The history of the controversy over whether or not to employ the nails in the production of sound is long.[48] The nineteenth century saw the recitalists, and as a result the tutors, divided over the issue. The leading no-nail player was Sor; the case for the use of nails was stated by Aguado:

We may play either with the nails or with the fleshy tips of the fingers of the right hand. For my part, I have always used my nails; nevertheless I resolved to cut my thumb nail after having heard (sic) my friend Mr. Sor play, and I congratulate myself on having followed his example. The impulse of the tip of the thumb on the bass notes produces full and agreeable tones. I retain the nails on the fore and middle fingers. My long experience may perhaps entitle me to give my opinion on this point. With the nails we obtain from the strings of the guitar a tone which does not resemble either that of the harp or that of the mandoline. In my opinion the guitar possesses a character which is distinct from that of other instruments: it is sweet, harmonious, pathetic, *sometimes* majestic: *it does not approach to the grandeur of the harp or the piano; but in revenge it possesses such delicate modifications of tone as renders it an almost* mysterious *instrument. For this reason I consider that it is desirable to twitch the strings with the nails; they produce a tone clear, metallic, diversified by much light and shade, and very sweet. It is as well to observe that it is not with the nails alone that I attack the strings; because in that case the tone would be coarse and disagreeable. The string is first touched by the left side of the tip of the finger, which then slides as far as the nail; it is this latter movement which gives clearness to the tone produced by the flesh. The nails should be rather flexible and very little above the extremities of the fingers. If they are too long, they impede the execution, because the string takes some time to get out of the nail. The velocity and clearness which have been remarked in passages of agility which I execute arise in a great measure from the employment of the nails; because, not being forced to seize upon the string, the action of the finger is more prompt.*[49]

One aspect of technique advocated in a number of tutors is the use of the left hand thumb to stop down notes on the bottom string. This was made posssible by the narrower fingerboard of the early nineteenth-century guitar; it would be an extremely awkward movement on the larger fingerboard of the modern instrument and is no longer employed. Giuliani makes use of this technique, indicating the notes to be stopped by the thumb by 'po', an abbreviation of *pollice*. The following extract is from the first variation of his Op. 128:

Example 9a: Giuliani Op. 128, extract from 1st Variation

In the third variation of the same work the thumb is used in higher positions:

Example 9b: Giuliani Op. 128, extract from 3rd Variation

It is clear that as yet no standard technique for the instrument had evolved. In England the approach to the instrument in Victorian times is typified by the solos performed by Madame Pratten in 1882.[50] Titles such as *Treue Liebe, Dreaming of Thee, Forgotten,* etc., etc. well express the level to which the guitar had sunk. It is hardly surprising to find the following announcement on the title-page of Madame Pratten's *Instructions for the Guitar tuned in E major:*

Owing to the limited sale of Guitar Music, Mme Pratten is obliged to charge FULL PRICE for her own Publications.

Once more it is to Spain that one must turn to trace the origin of the present interest in the guitar. Earlier traditions had been maintained by such men as Julian Arcas (1832–82), who toured widely before settling there. He was associated with Antonio Torres, and met the young Tárrega, who was to become the dominant personality of this period.

Tárrega – A Fresh Start

Francisco de Asis Tárrega Eixea was born in Villareal, Valencia in 1852 and died in Barcelona in 1909. Although he was acquainted with the guitar in his youth, he studied the piano at the Conservatorio in Madrid, where he won first prize for harmony and composition. However, it was the guitar he was to champion, and his public performances and teaching brought him great acclaim.

It was Tárrega who laid the foundations of modern technique. From his time the support of the instrument on the left leg became standard. This playing position is in part a consequence of the larger instrument initiated by Torres. The increase in body size of the guitar allows the player to adopt this posture in greater comfort than was possible with the smaller guitars of the early nineteenth century. Tárrega also established the use of the apoyando stroke. To incorporate this into right hand technique necessitates the abandonment of the practice of supporting the hand by resting the little finger on the table; in order to play either apoyando or tirando with any of the fingers as the texture of the music demands, the right hand must be poised over the strings with complete freedom (Plate 46f). A further Torres innovation may have contributed to this. The fingerboards of the small nineteenth-century guitars were either flush with the table, sometimes even when extended to the soundhole (Plate 36c), or at most *c.* 2 mm deep; the fingerboards of modern instruments are much deeper – 6–7 mm. With the modern bridge and saddle the height of the strings above the table is raised, which makes the supported position more awkward, particularly when complex music is performed. The deeper fingerboard can be seen in the side view of the Torres instrument of 1859[51] in the Museo Municipál de Música, Barcelona.

Tárrega differed from modern concert artists in one important respect; like Sor, he played without nails.

Tárrega travelled to Paris, London and Italy, but he was happiest in Spain. He composed a number of works for the guitar, mainly lightweight pieces of a romantic flavour that at times become a little too sentimental. His *Recuerdos de la Alhambra* is the most popular tremolo study yet written for the instrument. He overcomes the problem of a restricted texture by creating an attractive melodic movement that is well maintained. He further extended the guitar's repertory by transcribing a wide variety of music. Sometimes the choice was not a happy one, but some of his transcriptions were most successful. In particular, the piano pieces of Isaac Albeniz were regarded by the composer himself as sounding better on the guitar.

Among Tárrega's pupils were Miguel Llobet (1878–1938),[52] Maria Rita Brondi (1889–1941) and Emilio Pujol (*b.* 1886), who, by their recitals and musicological activities, have done much to establish the guitar on a firm footing. However, the real instigator of the present revival of interest in the guitar is another Spaniard – Andrés Segovia, (Plate 1) who, like his illustrious predecessor Luis Milán, is also a self-taught Maestro.

Chapter 6

The Twentieth Century:
A New Lease of Life

The present century is without doubt the most important in the history of the guitar. Until this century the progress of the instrument has been one of rise and fall; each period saw the guitar elevated for a while only to sink back once more to its traditional role as a popular instrument. Far from deprecating this, one can see in it a source of strength; to continue its life as a folk instrument, the guitar had to remain uncomplicated, and one can pay tribute to those many people who, because they were unambitious in their music-making, enabled the guitar to survive long enough to become the most active and the most important fretted instrument of today. This simplicity, however, meant that the early instruments were restricted in what they could achieve in the realm of art music. The careers of the four- and five-course guitars were short from this point of view, and the music they inspired, although of great historical interest, did not reach a sufficiently high standard to contribute a repertory adequate for today. The occasional works that are performed are in the nature of miniatures. The addition of the sixth string brought a much more ambitious exploration of the guitar's possibilities, but this was a false start to its modern existence, as enthusiasm could not be maintained in the face of conflicting musical trends, and the frail-voiced early nineteenth-century guitar had to await the stimulus of further structural improvements before attempting to assert its presence once ore. The significant contribution of the larger-scale works by them guitarist composers paved the way for the establishment of the modern repertory, but the total output of four centuries was not, by itself, enough for the modern recitalist. This is not so surprising when it is realized that the guitar is very much a late developer; consequently, at the beginning of the present century it could not rest on past achievements – it had to make its own future.

Tárrega had approached the problem of a limited repertory by adding transcriptions, mainly from the works of nineteenth-century composers. Segovia continued his precedent by delving into the music of earlier masters. He achieved great success with his performance of his transcription of the *Chaconne* from the *Second Partita in D Minor* for violin by Johann Sebastian Bach, much of whose music for violin and 'cello helped the guitar's quest for status. Further substantial music was to be found in his Suites for the lute, which, by Bach's time, had become quite a formidable instrument, having acquired too large a number of courses for it to continue as the most important fretted instrument. The last of the great lutenists, Sylvius Leopoldus Weiss, composed much interesting music for the Baroque lute. A contemporary of Bach, his music is similar in style, and he has achieved wider appreciation through the performance of his works on the guitar. The guitar, of course, has much in common with the lute and, with its more colourful range, it quite happily took over much of its music. At a time when the lute was cultivated only by a few enthusiasts, the great tradition of lutenist composers began to find expression on what had once been its scorned cousin. The music of the vihuelistas, of similar stature to that of the lute, also contributed to the guitar's second-hand repertory.

Keyboard music is more difficult to arrange for the guitar, but many of the works originally performed on the clavichord and harpsichord did not suffer when transcribed; the music of Frescobaldi, Rameau and Couperin began to be featured in recitals, its delicacy enhanced by the intimate guitar. Particularly suitable is the music of Domenico Scarlatti. Eighteenth-century Spanish music made a profound impression on the Italian composer, and the textures of his sonatas are often permeated by techniques that stem directly from the guitar:

Impressionistic polyphony is one of the oldest traditions of lute and guitar music (witness the sixteenth-century lute transcriptions of vocal and instrumental music). In a web of sound dominated by vertical harmony, the movement of voices and the entrances of voices and the entrances of subjects and imitations are indicated, but not fully carried out. No strict conduct of horizontal parts can be maintained. The sharpness of musical outline is blurred by the necessary breakings of chords by the impossibility of sounding all the voices simultaneously at the vertical points of consonance or dissonance at which they coincide. A whole technique of upwards and downwards

*and irregularly broken arpeggiation had to be developed in order to give the
impression that parts are sounding simultaneously whereas really they are
seldom together. Anyone who has heard Segovia play polyphonic music on
the guitar will know exactly what I mean.*

*Scarlatti's harpsichord music lies midway between the organ's real poly-
phony, with simultaneous sounding chords and voices, and the guitar's
impressionistic polyphony with broken chords and syncopated voices.*[1]

In the transcriptions of music from the past the guitar demonstrated its abilities; the viability of the instrument in the context of
twentieth-century music was another matter. Manuel de Falla had
decided views on this subject:

*Falla believes intensely in the future of the guitar. . . . But at this point
some reader may interrupt with a certain show of contempt: 'Future? I
should have thought it an instrument of the past; one with a past, at all
events!' It is true that, with us, the idea of 'playing on the Spanish
guitar' has somehow acquired a curiously disreputable significance, while the
instrument itself is – or was until the arrival of Andrés Segovia – regarded
as a piece of romantic stage furniture. 'No,' says Falla. 'Not at all!
Romantic times were precisely those in which the guitar was at its worst;
and then, of course, it spread all over Europe. It was made to play the sort
of music that other instruments played, but it was not really suitable for
nineteenth-century music, and so it dropped out. It is coming back again,
because it is peculiarly adapted for modern music.'*[2]

The twentieth-century repertory of original music of quality con-
ceived expressly for the guitar begins with a work by Falla himself –
Homenaje, written, in 1920, *Pour le Tombeau de Claude Debussy*. As well
as honouring the French composer, the piece fulfilled Falla's promise
to Miguel Llobet to write a work for the guitar. The story behind its
composition is told by Falla's biographer, Jaime Pahissa:

*He (Llobet) had repeatedly asked Falla to write a work for the guitar, and
Falla finally agreed. Debussy had recently died, and one day, at a concert in
Paris, Falla met Henri Prunières, who told him that he was going to
devote an issue of his Revue Musicale to Debussy's memory and asked
Falla to write an article for it. . . . Prunières' request troubled him.
Rather than write an article for it, he would have preferred to express his
admiration and affection for Debussy in music, but he did not know what*

kind of music to use. With regard to the music, he had only one fixed idea, that it should end with Debussy's Soirée dans Grenade. *Then it occurred to him that he could make it a work for the guitar, thus satisfying Llobet at the same time. So, on his way through Barcelona, when returning from Paris to Granada, he told Llobet of his decision.*

Falla set himself to study the guitar in order to appreciate its technique fully, as he had done with other instruments in accordance with Dukas' advice. A fortnight later, to his great surprise, Llobet received the Hommage pour le Tombeau de Debussy.³

It is ironic that Falla expressed his tribute on the guitar, as Debussy had, in fact, wanted to write for the instrument, but Llobet is supposed to have dissuaded him from so doing.⁴ Whether or not this was so, it is to be regretted that nothing came of Debussy's desire, as transcriptions of some of his works sound well on the guitar.

Falla planned to write another work for the guitar, *La Tertulia*, which was 'to convey the atmosphere of those musical evenings popular in nineteenth-century homes, at which one young lady would play, another sing and yet another recite.'⁵ Unfortunately this did not become a reality, and the *Homenaje* was his sole contribution to the guitar's literature.

Llobet introduced the guitar to a wider audience by his recital tours, but it was to be the fate of Andrés Segovia to establish the guitar internationally. No small feat, but the Maestro has applied himself most diligently to the work this entailed, and pride of place in the twentieth century is undoubtedly his.

The Achievement of Andrés Segovia

Segovia's task was two-fold: to extend the repertory of the guitar and present it to as wide a public as possible, the aim of both labours being to establish the guitar finally as a respected instrument. Born in Linares in Jaén on 21 February 1893,⁶ Segovia began his musical studies in Granada. He rejected other instruments in favour of the guitar, which he studied on his own; it has always been his proud claim that he has been his own pupil and master. Tárrega extended the technique of the instrument, but Segovia refined it. His right-hand approach is different from Tárrega's; the latter's rather severe turn of the wrist brings the first finger at a right-angle to the strings, whereas in the more relaxed Segovia position it is the third finger that adopts this angle. In the production of sound Segovia uses either the nails alone or in combination with the fingertips, depending on the texture of the music.[7] The earlier advances in technique made by the vihuelistas are thus completed by these latter-day distinguished Spaniards.

Segovia must have been a hard task-master as he was sufficiently advanced by the time he was fourteen to give his first recital. He went on to tour Spain and then South America. His début in Paris in 1924 was before a distinguished audience that included Falla and Albert Roussel, whose *Segovia* was first performed on this auspicious occasion; the stately movement of this work well reflects the dignity Segovia had achieved for and through the guitar.

From this time, Segovia was to extend his recital tours, and it would now be difficult to name a country where he has not performed. He can be justly proud of his achievement; many of his pupils are concert artists in their own right and, through their teaching in conservatoires throughout the world, they are maintaining and establishing more securely present interest in the guitar. This has been facilitated by the growing body of original music for the instrument, and here again Segovia has taken a leading role; by his sensitive performances he attracted composers to the possibilities of expression on the guitar, and its literature began to be extended as never before.

In Spain Falla's lead was followed by Joaquin Turina (1882–1949) and Federico Moreno Torroba (*b*. 1891), who began to produce works in collaboration with Segovia. Their idiom leaves no doubt about their nationality. Turina's *Fandanguillo* and Torroba's *Suite Castellana*, both published in 1926, forcefully express native traditions in their strong rhythmic movement. Torroba sustained a dramatic effect in *Nocturno*, which appeared in the same year, but a calmer mood is established in *Preludio* (1928) and the very lyrical *Burgalesa* (1928). Humour pervades his *Serenata Burlesca*, another 1928 publication, and his early period of guitar compositions is brought to a close by *Pièces Charactéristiques* (1931), a collection of six pieces, whose titles express their content: *Preambulo, Oliveras, Melodia, Los Mayos, Albada* and *Panorama*.

Turina continued his output with *Ráfaga* (1930), a descriptive piece portraying a gust of wind. The two movements *Garrotin* and *Soleares*, which constitute his *Hommage à Tárrega* (1935), are full of flamenco effects and can well be described as formal examples of this genre. His most ambitious composition for the guitar was the *Sonata* (1932), whose texture is similar to that of his shorter works. The very popular *Sonatina* (1953) by Torroba is a more varied work, and its attractive themes continue the charm that is evident in his less ambitious pieces.

Segovia's visits to South America also inspired new music. The Mexican composer Manuel Ponce (1882–1948) responded by producing a greater number of extended works than Turina and Torroba had achieved. In some of his sonatas, tribute is paid to the guitar's past, while in others the writing is in a more modern idiom. *Sonata Romantica*, subtitled *Hommage à Franz Schubert, qui aimait la guitare*, and *Sonata Clásica, Hommage à Fernando Sor*, evoke a nineteenth-century atmosphere, while *Sonata III* and *Thème Varié et Finale* return to the present. In these latter two works, Ponce demonstrates his ability to create intriguing textures with unexpected melodic movements and rhythmic subtlety. This is also true of his *Twelve Preludes*, but he is not without tenderness, as *Chanson*, the second movement of *Sonata III*, demonstrates. These works come from the twenties; a later work, *Sonata Meridional*, is suffused with southern warmth and gaiety, qualities also to be found in his *Concierto del Sur*, which was given its first performance in Montevideo in 1941 by Segovia.

The contribution from South America is most notable for the music of Brazil's Heitor Villa-Lobos (1887–1959). Segovia has described his first meeting with him in 1924, on which occasion, although he was fearful for his guitar in the composer's unpractised hands, he recognized the freshness of the music he struggled to perform.[8] His *Douze Études* (1929), the first to be written for the instrument by a non-specialist, not only serve to prepare the guitarist for the more demanding textures of modern music, but at times attain a beauty of expression that has guaranteed a permanent place in recitalists' programmes. The *Cinq Préludes* (1940) in the main make great use of a technique encountered in the first of the twelve studies. A chord is moved up and down the fingerboard and sounded against open strings acting as a pedal point within an arpeggio pattern. Although apparently a simple procedure, the result is most effective. Villa-Lobos's music can only be described as eclectic; it comprises traditional Brazilian forms, as in *Chôros No. 1 for guitar*, the first of a number composed for various combinations of instruments, and works with strong European influence, explicitly acknowledged in the title of *Bachianas Brasileiras*, the fifth of which, originally composed for voice and eight cellos, was re-arranged by Villa-Lobos for voice and guitar.

Villa-Lobos, as Ponce had done, produced a guitar concerto, but the honour of composing the first of the present century (Giuliani had shown the way in the nineteenth) goes to Mario Castelnuovo-Tedesco (1895–1968),[9] whose *Concerto in D* appeared in 1939. Prior to this, he had followed Ponce's precedent by paying homage to earlier personalities connected with the guitar: *Capriccio Diabolico, Ommagio a Paganini* and *Sonata, Ommagio a Boccherini* (1935). The latter is in four movements, its rousing opening changing to an atmosphere of introspection in the second movement, which is sustained in the graceful *Minuet*, but broken by the fiery finale, *Vido ed energico*. The romantic fluency betrayed by Castelnuovo-Tedesco continues in *Tarantella* and *Aranci in Fiore* and is given full expression in his *Concerto*, the simple but attractive themes of which make no great demands on the listener. Much the same can be said for his *Quintet for Guitar and Strings* (1953), one of the few modern works to feature the guitar in chamber music.

Castelnuovo-Tedesco was an Italian, and a further widening of the guitar's vocabulary came with the music of Alexander Tansman (*b.* 1897), who is of Polish extraction. His *Cavatina* won the first prize of the *Concours international* of the Accademia Chigiana in Siena in 1951, and its four movements, *Preludio, Sarabande, Scherzino* and *Barcarola*, were given a more spirited finish by the addition, at Segovia's suggestion, of *Danza Pomposa*. The Suite is most attractive in the rhythmic variety of the livelier movements set against the languorous charm of the *Sarabande* and *Barcarola*. Tansman's other guitar compositions include *Trois Pièces – Canzonetta, Alla Polacca* and *Berceuse d'Orient* – and, as might be expected, a *Mazurka*.

Spanish traditions were continued by Joaquín Rodrigo (*b.* 1902). A version for guitar of *Sarabanda Lejana*, originally for strings, is dedicated 'to the vihuela of Luis Milán', while in later compositions he honours modern performers. The *Concierto de Aranjuez* (1939) was written for Regino Sainz de la Maza, and, ever since its enthusiastic reception, it has remained an extremely popular work. *Por los Campos de España* (1958) contains two studies, *En los Trigales* for Narciso Yepes and *Entre Olivares* for Manuel Lopez Ramos. *Tres Piezas Españolas* was dedicated to Segovia, as was Rodrigo's second work for guitar and orchestra, *Fantasia para un Gentilhombre* (1954). The composer has said of the work:

*I thought that the only thing worthy of Segovia would be to place him to-
gether with another great guitarist and composer, born in the XVII century,
a gentleman in the court of Philip IV, Gaspar Sanz. I consulted Segovia
himself, who approved the plan, but not without first warning me of the
difficulties of its realization, saying that I would have to work with themes
which were very short. Right away Victoria, my wife, selected for me from
the book of Gaspar Sanz a short number of themes which we judged appropriate to form a sort of suite-fantasia and which we very soon decided to call*
Fantasia para un Gentilhombre, *playing thus on the names of these two
nobles of the guitar: Gaspar Sanz and Andrés Segovia, in his turn Gentleman of the Guitar of our days.*[10]

Segovia clearly emerges as the dominant figure of the first half of
the twentieth century. As a result of his efforts, the guitar has become
well established in the United States, the Middle East, the Far East
and Australia as well as in all the countries of Europe. It can now be
regarded as a truly international instrument, and this contact with so
many different cultures should prove to be a most fruitful union as
composers in these many countries turn to the guitar. In this further
stage, Segovia has played a part, albeit indirectly. He is happiest in
the performance of romantic music, and it is natural that the works
produced under his influence do not venture too far into textures that
reflect modern trends. However, he has also inspired a new genera-
tion of guitarists, and as they in their turn sought new music, they
turned to composers who have most decidedly broadened the spec-
trum of twentieth-century guitar music. England is fortunate to have
two such guitarists of high calibre – Julian Bream and John Williams.
(Plate 46f.) Of the two, John Williams owes a greater debt to Segovia.

The Guitar in England

Segovia held master classes for a number of years in Italy, at the
Accademia Musicale Chigiana in Siena. With him as *maestro-
collaboratore* was Alirio Diaz, the Venezuelan virtuoso. It was here
that Williams received much of his training, his progress being so
phenomenal that he became the first of the students there to be
invited to give a full recital. Born in 1941 in Australia, Williams began
the study of the guitar at the age of six. He was taught by his father,
Leonard, who later established the Spanish Guitar Centre in London,
the first institution in this country to offer classical guitar tuition. It
was necessary for John to continue his guitar studies in Siena, as the

instrument was not on the curriculum at the Royal College of Music, where he received his general musical education. This situation was remedied in 1960, when Williams himself was invited to become Professor of the guitar there.

At his début at the Wigmore Hall in 1958, Williams presented a maturity of command over the guitar that was most impressive. The fluency of his performance has set a very high standard in England, and this, allied to his intelligent musicality, has given him a place among international recitalists. He has made successful tours of the United States, the Soviet Union, Japan and Europe.

Stephen Dodgson (b. 1924) has become associated with Williams in his compositions for the guitar and has been successful in expressing his very individual ideas without allowing the instrument's Iberian heritage to affect his musical thinking. In 1965 this philosophy was given expression in the preface to *Twenty Studies for the Guitar*, composed by Dodgson in collaboration with Hector Quine, Professor of the guitar at the Royal Academy of Music:

> *The classical studies, with their attractive but predictable patterns, seldom do enough to develop the guitar student's general musical ability. Nor do they extend his powers of reading, his musical imagination or his technical curiosity very far on the way towards the complex rhythmic shapes and unusual sonorities he will assuredly meet in any music of the present century.*
>
> *The studies were written in a spirit of exploration, and in the conviction that the gap between most guitarist's daily musical fare and the age in which they live needs something to fill it. We hope these pieces may go some way toward providing this.*

The Dodgson-Quine studies take an important step forward from those by Villa-Lobos. In attempting them, the guitarist is immediately aware of a feeling of unfamiliarity; the notes do not fall readily under the fingers as the successive phrases present changes of texture and unexpected rhythms. This is in sharp contrast with much previous guitar music. The practice of adopting a basic movement that proceeds inexorably to the end of the piece is the hallmark of a great amount of nineteenth-century guitar music, and at times it appears in extended sections of the Villa-Lobos studies, though in modern garb.

A precedent for this shifting attitude towards writing for the guitar can be found in Frank Martin's *Quatre Pièces Brèves*. Although written in 1933, this work's style is out of step with the general tone of guitar music of the period. The fact that it has only recently received a wide hearing is most indicative of the change of climate. Dodgson himself has helped this development gain momentum through his growing number of compositions for the instrument: *Partita for Guitar*, a *Concerto* and, his most recent work, *Fantasy-Divisions* (1969).

Other composers have not been slow in consolidating the beginnings of what might be termed the northern repertory. Here, the most influential figure without doubt has been Julian Bream, whose depth of musicianship has brought him to the fore as one of the leading performers of the day. Born in 1933, he was drawn to the guitar at the age of twelve. His technique has been in the main self-acquired and, as Williams did, he studied at the Royal College of Music without being able to pursue the guitar there. In spite of these difficulties, his talent was such that he attained a standard of performance that ensures he is in constant demand throughout the world. Bream is also a virtuoso lutenist, having enriched the instrument by bringing to it his experience on the guitar; no doubt the reverse has been true.

The music that has appeared in Bream's wake reveals a range of complexity that at times becomes most demanding on both performer and listener. A work of immediate appeal is Malcolm Arnold's *Guitar Concerto*, its attraction not being diminished by such a direct approach. The instrument's Spanish associations are avoided, but its more recent jazz background is introduced in the second movement. Bream has commented:

> *The Lento, which provides the central framework of the Concerto, was written as an elegy in memory of the famous French guitarist Django Reinhardt – a special hero of both Malcolm and myself. Its mood is reflected in a finely dressed blues, briefly interrupted by a vivace section.*

Lennox Berkeley's *Sonatina*, written for Bream in 1958, exploits many of the guitar's effects, tremolo, pizzicato, open string pedals and rasgueado, which results in a work of great liveliness, tempered by the ghostly quality of the second movement. Some of the standard possibilities also appear in Benjamin Britten's *Nocturnal* (1964), but in order to achieve the desired sonororities, these were not enough. New effects appeared, and the consequent textural difficulties extend the performer to the full. Not only is his technique put to the test; the nature of the work also demands high interpretative abilities. It is based on John Dowland's song *Come, heavy sleep*, which is an apt choice, leading as it does to the happy situation of England's first lutenist being re-expressed by the present foremost lutenist on the guitar. Britten adopts the unusual procedure of reserving the statement of the theme until the end of the work, but this is an ideal position, as it resolves the emotional intensity of the earlier sections. A calm opening gives way to most disturbing sections, which are appropriately headed *Very Agitated*, *Restless*, and *Uneasy*. A quieter section follows, but the excitement returns as the *Passacaglia* reaches its climax, which is relieved by the tranquillity of the theme. The *Nocturnal* stands out from the more adventurous modern music for the guitar, and it must be regarded as the greatest work yet produced for the instrument.

Britten has also used the guitar most effectively in his settings of *Songs from the Chinese* (1958). The repertory for voice and guitar has received new impetus through the performances of Peter Pears accompanied by Julian Bream and the partnership of the late Wilfrid Brown and John Williams. The recent works in this medium demonstrate the suitability of the guitar's intimacy and wide range of colour in underlining the various moods expressed by the verses. One can cite here Lennox Berkeley's *Songs of the Half-Light*, Raymond Warren's *The Pity of Love*, Sir William Waltons *Anon in Love*, Stephen Dodgson's *Poems by John Clare*, Roberto Gerhard's *Cantares*, Thea Musgrave's *Five Love Songs* – an impressive list, and one looks forward to further settings in this healthy reaction against the nineteenth-century practice of resting content with a simple chordal or arpeggio accompaniment.

Any assessment of modern guitar music is made difficult by the fact that it is still in the process of evolution. The task is not lightened by the increasing output of music for the instrument from many parts of the world. A further factor is that one no longer has the situation of one composer writing exclusively for the medium, as was very often the case in the past; it is now a question of many composers including the guitar among the instruments they write for, and a full appreciation of current guitar music should take into account the style and general musical thought of the composers concerned. Consequently a complete evaluation must await some future historian. One can, however, illustrate some of the textures that have appeared in the present century.

In general the most successful recent guitar-writing exploits the instrument's contrapuntal possibilities rather than its traditional harmonic vocabulary. In other words, it has continued the tradition of pseudo-polyphonic writing established on the vihuela and lute.

Example 10: Opening of the Third Movement of Lennox Berkeley's *Sonatina for Guitar*, Op. 51.

Although this produces what appears to be a thin texture, the reality of performance creates a fuller sound, as both open strings and stopped down notes last longer than their notated value. This is true of the larger part of guitar, and lute, music. It is particularly evident when an arpeggio pattern is established through a held-down chord:

Example 11: Opening of Study No. 20 by Stephen Dodgson and Hector Quine

This is much more than a series of semiquavers; all the notes continue to sound until struck again with the right-hand fingers, so that the forward movement is spiced with dissonance.

The use of open strings acting as a pedal point has often been a feature of guitar music, and the present is no exception:

Example 12: Extract from *Etude No. 11* by Villa-Lobos

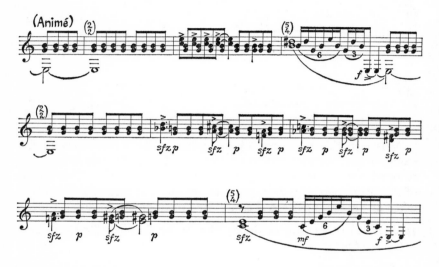

Throughout this section of the study, the melody in thirds, played on the fourth and fifth strings, rises and falls past the repeated second and third strings played open, and produces subtle harmonic shifts. One suspects that such writing owes more to the nature of the instrument than to the composer's imagination.

The internal pedal that appears in the polymetric third section of Britten's *Nocturnal* includes stopped notes, but these are not allowed to restrict melodic movement, as the player locates the necessary notes in a higher position:

Example 13: Opening of III *Restless* from *Nocturnal* by Benjamin Britten, Op. 70

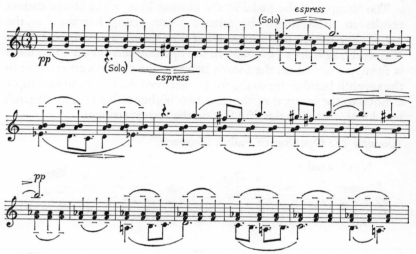

In *Quasi una Marcia*, which appears later in the same work, Britten uses the open strings in a reiterated rhythm against a melody in double octaves on the outside strings. The internal pedal starts A and D (fifth and fourth strings), proceeds to D and G (fourth and third), then G and B (third and second) until finally all four inside strings appear:

Example 14: Extract from *Quasi una Marcia* (*Nocturnal*)

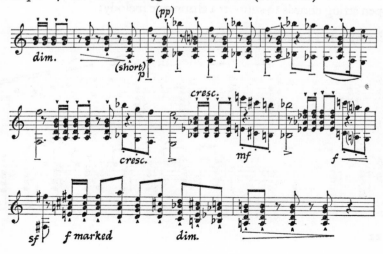

The double octave *portamento* is played by Julian Bream with great panache.

The 'escape' of the pedal in the closing bars of the above extract results in what might be termed 'open string harmony' – the use of chords built on fourths rather than thirds. These appear, most effectively, in Falla's *Homenaje*. In the opening section the movement is firmly anchored on the fourth between the two lowest strings; in the seventh bar the rise to the fourth between A and D can be simply a move to the interval of the next two higher strings or, as fingered by Llobet, played at the fifth fret on the lowest strings:

Example 15: Opening of Falla's *Homenaje*

(*Sounds marked* ✕ *must be accented according to the nuances and very lightly held.*)

Plainte, the third of Frank Martin's *Quatre Pièces Brèves*, uses fuller open string chords to support a chromatic melody:

Example 16: Extract from Plainte

Some of the above effects are intrinsic to the guitar and are playable with no great difficulty. However, both Bream and Williams have commented on the technical demands of some of the music written for them. This is a most healthy sign, as it means that composers are not allowing their ideas to be restricted by the instrument; in this way, platitudes will be avoided, and the guitar can only be enriched.

The music that has been considered in the above partial survey has gone a long way towards filling the lacuna that was very evident at the beginning of the present century. An examination of recital programmes reveals this widening of the repertory, but one is also very much aware of the continued need for transcriptions to add musical weight. Critics have not been slow to attack the shortcomings, and, as well as eulogies, one can come across such harsh comments as:

> *When one short, superficial, banal and even vulgar item follows another, each seemingly more insistent on harmonic clichés and predictable* rubatos *than the one before, no amount of technical persuasion can rescue the listener from a sort of Spanish boredom.*

and the following, which contains a more serious charge:

> *Although guitar recitals are featured regularly at the Wigmore Hall this season, it seems that even imagination and mastery of fiendish technical problems hardly compensate for the instrument's crippling musical limitations.*

Adverse criticism and the guitar are old friends. Sometimes the criticism has been justified and, if it is constructive, this is all to the good. However, one cannot help feeling that there are occasions when the attacks are misguided, and more is expected than the instrument can provide. One does not dismiss the bowed and wind instruments on account of their essentially monodic quality. Similarly, one must not expect the harmonic possibilities and volume of a piano when considering the guitar. It is essential to evaluate the instrument on its own terms, and explore what it is capable of achieving.

The solo instrument has gained tremendously in the present century, but many avenues remain to be explored. The guitar has been little featured in chamber music; its range of colour invites a juxtaposition against contrasting timbres, and it would be pleasant to see this potential realized. The duo form, so splendidly established by Ida Presti and Alexandre Lagoya, as yet lacks the repertory of stimulating music it deserves. The addition of a second guitar avoids the restrictions present in writing for the solo instrument[11] and opens up great musical possibilities. Ida Presti's death in 1967 robbed the guitar world of one of its outstanding performers; however, her inspiration lives on in the growing number of duettists.

Present and Future

The rise of the guitar in the present century is no new phenomenon; its history has been one of similar periods of popularity, but the current vogue has achieved a stability that implies permanence. Developments in the instrument itself have played an important part, but other factors have contributed. The quickening of communications and the innovations of gramophone records, radio and television have brought the guitar before a much wider audience. Modern research has resulted in the revival of early music, and the reaction against the nineteenth-century desire for volume has meant that the guitar's intimate voice has been listened to with greater sympathy. The past waves of popularity suggest a latent force that is always ready to turn to the guitar, and in the present century the instrument has continued to attract the amateur.

The nineteenth-century emphasized the gulf between the amateur and the virtuoso performer, and it was then necessary for the guitarists to compose at two levels. Much of the music of the present century requires an even higher standard of performance, and the amateur, while being able to manage some of the repertory, has not been served as well as he might have been. A work such as Francis Poulenc's *Sarabande*, composed for Ida Presti in 1960, is a refreshing change for the not very advanced performer, and it would be pleasant to see much more music that is worth while and yet does not demand too many years of practice. However, the amateur can explore an extremely wide range of music through transcriptions as well as original works. The problems that have faced the recitalists are not his, and he can pursue with profit the music of five centuries.

England has been tardy in giving recognition to the guitar. The Spanish Guitar Centre was not established in London until 1952, and it has been pointed out how our leading virtuosi had to acquire their art with no facilities for study in this country. The growth of specialist teaching centres throughout the country has improved matters, and education authorities are gradually recognizing the benefits of guitar tuition in schools, not merely as a vehicle for strumming but as a serious pursuit. John Gavall, who has done much pioneer work in fostering the use of the guitar in schools, wrote hopefully in 1954:

> *In the schools which have so far begun to experiment with it, the response from children has been highly enthusiastic. Many hitherto apathetic subjects have been galvanised into taking an active interest in music, from actual building of their own instruments to composition of simple songs, and the formation of small ensembles. It is reasonable to suppose that, together with the increase in the public for professional performances on the guitar, an even larger movement in its favour will soon become perceptible in the fields of general education and of amateur music-making in the home.*[12]

A more recent article on the value of the guitar in education succinctly states the reason why the situation is still far from ideal:

> *The main problem confronting all concerned with guitar tuition is the shortage of instructors.*[13]

The inspiration of the recitalists results in an ever increasing number of aspiring players; an established background of informed teaching is a basic necessity.

The guitar now cuts through many musical strata, and it is important to distinguish the various styles of performance. The rise of the classical approach coincided with the emergence of the modern instrument in the second half of the nineteenth century; the earlier performance of art music on the guitar leaned heavily on lute technique. The aspect of technique that most marks the break with the past is the extent to which the right hand has been developed. This has come with the guitar's exploration of music of more complex texture than that of its traditional repertory, and both Tárrega and Segovia realized that if the guitar was to accommodate the music it deserved, its technique should be extended accordingly.

This development must be seen against the constant background of the guitar being used for accompaniment, a role it is still filling. In this context a number of offshoot guitars have appeared, ranging from the flamenco guitar to the ubiquitous electric guitar, and these, too, have developed their own techniques. Some of these techniques involve the use of a plectrum to produce sounds, thus limiting the musical possibilities. When the right hand fingers are used, the position of the hands reveals the extent of the demands of the music on the performer. In short, the simpler the music, the more casual the approach can be. The classical guitarist must consequently adopt a very strict posture; only in this way can he achieve the full development of the fingers that will allow him to project the music he performs with conviction.

The cultivation of such a technique is no easy matter. Unfortunately this is not yet appreciated sufficiently widely, and much that passes for classical instruction is most harmful in establishing an incorrect approach. Modern guitar technique is *sui generis* and it cannot be acquired through any of the other guitar styles. There is no doubt that the guitar is a difficult instrument to play well; now that it has become the established instrument after its many skirmishes with the lute, it has not only inherited the lute's traditional difficulties, but also progressed to an even more demanding level. As such, it needs careful fostering, and this can be achieved even with the very young,[14] who very often take up the guitar as an instrument of immediate appeal. The importance of such activity cannot be overemphasized; through it the guitar will cease to be regarded with surprise or wonder and finally become accepted as playing a normal part in the world of music. It surely deserves this after so many centuries of struggle.

Notes and References

Chapter one (pp. 5–23)

1 Emilio Pujol: *Monumentos de la Música Española*, vol. VII, 1949, p. 6, fn. 4.

2 Anthony Baines: 'Fifteenth-century instruments in Tinctoris's De Inventione et Usu Musicae 1487', *Galpin Society Journal*, vol. III, 1950.

3 *The Civilization of the Renaissance in Italy* (1860), transl. by S. G. C. Middlemore, London, 1965, p. 69.

4 In addition to the instruments considered here, further references can be found in Victor Ravizza: *Die Instrumentale Ensemble von 1400–1550 in Italien*, Bern and Stuttgart, 1970; and in Valentin Denis: *De Muziekinstrumenten in de Nederlanden en in Italië naar hun Afbeelding in de 15e-eeuwsche Kunst*, Louvain, 1944.

5 A number of fifteenth-century fiddles betray features of plucked instruments; cf. for example Denis, *op. cit.* fig. 3, a fiddle with a bridge fixed to the table, and a central soundhole as well as C-holes, and fig. 11, a fiddle which has four C-holes, a tailpiece, a central rose and the bent-back peg-box of the lute.

6 Bezalel Narkiss: *Hebrew Illuminated Manuscripts*, Jerusalem, 1969, p. 156; the complete folio appears as Pl.58.

7 John Ward: *The Vihuela de Mano and its Music*, unpublished Ph.D. thesis, New York University, 1953, contains a section devoted to the viola da mano, p. 60 ff.

8 *The Autobiography of Benvenuto Cellini*, transl. George Bull, Harmondsworth, 1956, pp. 18, 20.

9 Paolo Cortese: *De cardinalatu libri tres* (1510), extract transl. by Nino Pirotta, 'Music and Cultural Tendencies in fifteenth-century Italy', *Journal of the American Musicological Society*, vol. XIX, No. 2, Summer, 1966; the awkwardness of 'uniformity' as a translation of *similitudo* is lessened if it is thought of as 'lack of tonal variety'. In the commentary to his translation, p. 157, Pirotta describes an

audition arranged so that he could compare the sound of the lute with that of the vihuela; he preferred the 'much richer variety of nuanced effects' of the lute.

10 John Ward: *op. cit.*, p. 60.

11 Some early fiddles also had four roses and similarly decorated tables, see Denis, *op. cit.*, figs. 1, 8 and 9.

12 Michael Prynne: 'A surviving Vihuela de Mano', *Galpin Society Journal*, vol. XVI, 1963.

13 Edmond van der Straeten: *La Musique aux Pays Bas*, vol. 7, p. 251.

14 Gilbert Chase: *The Music of Spain*, 2nd revised ed., New York, 1959, p. 53.

15 Detailed accounts of the two methods of construction can be found in Irving Sloane, *Classic Guitar Construction*, New York, 1966, which describes the Spanish method, and in Donald McLeod and Robert Welford, *The Classical Guitar*, *Design and Construction*, Leicester and New Jersey, 1971, which describes the dovetail method.

16 Baines: *loc. cit.* This instrument has been regarded as a mandore by Karl Geiringer, 'Der Instrumentenname "Quinterne" und die mittelalterlichen Bezeichnungen der Gitarre, Mandola und des Colascione', *Archiv für Musikwissenschaft*, May 1924. Although like the lute in body, this instrument's tuning in fourths and fifths does not seem to be related to that of the lute. Geiringer's table (p. 110) equates vihuela with guitar in the sixteenth century, but it omits *guitarre, guiterne* and their variants. The use of these names for guitar-like instruments cannot be overlooked, and as one of the sixteenth-century guitar-types has so much in common with the fifteenth-century lute, Tinctoris's term is taken as referring to such an instrument. The present writer does not hold the view that 'guitar' and 'vihuela' are synonymous.

17 Prologo al lector, f. 4r.

18 Juan Bermudo: *Declaración de Instrumentos Musicales*, 1555, f. 96.

19 Fantasia XI.

20 Daniel Heartz: 'An Elizabethan Tutor for the Guitar', *Galpin Society Journal*, vol. XVI, 1963.

21 Bermudo: *op. cit.*, f. 28v.

22 This isolated tuning by Cellier has been variously interpreted. It has been regarded by Daniel Heartz (*op. cit.*, p. 16) as a skeleton tuning, which he completes by adding a further string an octave below the fifth and two more in unison with the second and third strings. (Heartz comments incorrectly that 'One more fourth, added next time at the bottom rather than the top, will produce the interval tuning of the classic guitar'.) Sylvia

Murphy ('The Tuning of the Five-course Guitar', *Galpin Society Journal*, vol. XXIII, 1970, p. 50) argues that Cellier intended to show that the two strings of the fifth course were tuned in unison. The lack of bourdons on the fourth and fifth courses of the Baroque guitar signifies plucked music as opposed to strummed chords, and one is suspicious of such a tuning in the late sixteenth century as there is no evidence that the music played on the instrument was polyphonic. Luis de Briceño (*Metodo mui facilissimo para aprender a tañer la guitarra a lo Español*, Paris, 1626, f. 5), gives a tuning that has the fourth and fifth courses without bourdons – aa d'd' gg bb e'. His book contains only strummed chords, but as Hélène Charnassé has pointed out in considering Briceño's tuning ('Sur l'Accord de la Guitare', *Recherches sur la Musique Française Classique*, vol. VII, 1967, pp. 30–31) 'although there is no question of strings being tuned at the octave in this text, the transcription of the tablature given at the beginning of the work for reference is musically valid only if the two lowest courses are tuned thus' and her example corresponds to the tuning given by Amat.

23 Juan Carlos Amat: *Guitarra Española*, 1639, pp. 1–2.

24 Nicolas Doizi de Velasco: *Nuevo Modo de Cifra para tañer la Guitarra*, 1640, p. 2.

25 Gaspar Sanz: *Instrucción de Música sobre la Guitarra Española*, 1674, Prlogue f. 6.

26 Amat: *op. cit.* Prologue *al lector*: 'called Spanish, because it has been more welcome (*recibida*) in this country than in others.'

27 Isabel Pope Conant: 'Vicente Espinel as a Musician', *Studies in the Renaissance*, vol. V. 1958, pp. 142ff.

28 *Discours non plus mélancoliques que divers, de choses mêmement qui appartiennent à notre France*, extract on fretting reprinted in J. B. Weckerlin, *Nouveau Musicana*, 1890, pp. 103–120; the work has been attributed to various authors – Bonaventure des Périers, Elie Vinet, Pelletier du Mans.

29 Bermudo: *op. cit.*, f. 102.

30 Bermudo: *op. cit.*, f. 108v.

31 Bermudo: *op. cit.*, f. 107v.

32 J. Murray Barbour: *Tuning and Temperament*, 1953, p. 166.

33 Franz Jahnel: *Die Gitarre und ihr Bau*, 1963, p. 152.

34 The constant is given as 17.835 by McLeod and Welford, *op. cit.*, p. 11.

35 Ward: *op. cit.*, p. 35.

36 Doizi de Velasco: *op. cit.*, pp. 12–13.

37 François Lesure: 'La Guitare en France au XVIe Siècle', *Musica Disciplina* IV, 1950, p. 188; see also 'La facture instrumentale à

Paris au Seizième Siècle', *Galpin Society Journal*, vol. VII, 1954 and vol. X, 1957 by the same author.

38 van der Straeten: *op. cit.*, vol. VI, p. 516.

39 Marin Mersenne: *Harmonie Universelle*, 1636, *The Books on Instruments, 2nd Book of Stringed Instruments, Proposition XIV: To explain the shape, tuning, tablature and the playing of the guitar*, transl. R. E. Chapman, 1957.

40 Width and depth measurements are as follows: the widths are across the table in the order upper bout – waist – lower bout; the progression in depth is from the upper to the lower part of the body. Measurements for the guitars in the Ashmolean Collection are taken from David D. Boyden: *Catalogue of the Hill Collection . . . . in the Ashmolean Museum*, 1969, and those in the Victoria and Albert Museum from Anthony Baines: *Victoria and Albert Museum Catalogue*, vol. II, 1968.

41 quoted by Constant Pierre: *Les Facteurs d'Instruments de Musique*, 1893, pp. 66–67.

42 A. Bruni: *Un Inventaire sous la Terreur*, Paris, 1890.

43 Robert Fissore: *Les Maîtres Luthiers*, 4th ed. *c.* 1890.

44 Constant Pierre: *loc. cit.*

45 Nicholas Bessaraboff: *Ancient European Musical Instruments*, 1964, No. 256, p. 242, Fig. 45.

46 Michel Corrette: *Les Dons d'Apollon*, 1763, Book 1, p. 5.

47 Gunther Hellwig: 'Joachim Tielke', *Galpin Society Journal*, XVIII, 1964.

48 quoted by Johannes Wolf: *Handbuch der Notationskunde*, 1919, vol. II, p. 167.

49 *Guitar Review*, No. 32, 1969, p. 17.

50 Boyden: *op. cit.*, p. 45.

Chapter Two (pp. 24–40)

1 Diana Poulton: 'Notes on Some Differences between the Lute and the Vihuela and their Music' *The Consort*, No. 16, July 1959.

2 Bermudo: *op. cit.*, f. 29v.

3 Bermudo: *op. cit.*, f. 30.

4 Bermudo: *op. cit.*, f. 30v.

5 Pero Mexia: History of Charles V (1551, reprinted 1918), quoted by John Roberts: 'The death of Guzman', *The Lute Society Journal*, vol. X, 1968, p. 36.

6 Bermudo: *op. cit.*, f. 99v.

7 Higini Angles: 'Latin Church Music on the Continent, 3 – Spain and Portugal', *New Oxford History of Music*, vol. IV, 1969, p. 379.

8 Gerald Brenan: *The Literature of the Spanish People*, 1963, p. 121ff.

9 J. B. Trend: *Luis Milan and the Vihuelistas*, 1925, p. 46.

10 Nigel Fortune: 'Solo Song and Cantata', *New Oxford History of Music*, vol. IV, p. 129 and John Ward: *op. cit.*, p. 95ff.

11 Trend: *The Music of Spanish History to 1600*, 1926, p. 105.

12 Bermudo: *op. cit.*, f. 96v.

13 *Die Musik in Geschichte und Gegenwart*, 5, entry 'Gorlier', cols. 533–4 (François Lesure).

14 Thoinot Arbeau: *Orchesography* (1588) trans. Cyril W. Beaumont, 1925, p. 112.

15 Daniel Heartz: 'An Elizabethan Tutor for the Guitar', *Galpin Society Journal*, vol. XVI 1963.

16 *M.G.G.* 9, entry 'Morlaye', cols. 588–9 (François Lesure)

17 *Orchesography*, p. 86.

18 *M.G.G.* 2, entry 'Brayssing', cols. 241–2 (François Lesure).

19 Heartz: 'Parisian Music Publishing under Henry II', *The Musical Quarterly*, October, 1960.

20 Heartz: *op. cit.*, p. 459.

21 Heartz: 'An Elizabethan Tutor', p. 17.

22 van der Straeten: *op. cit.*, vol. II, p. 372.

23 F. G. Emmerson: *Sir William Petre*, 1961, p. 210.

24 Walter L. Woodfill: *Musicians in English Society from Elizabeth to Charles I*, 1953, p. 276.

25 reproduced in Heartz: 'An Elizabethan Tutor', Plate IIa.

26 Denis Stevens: *The Mulliner Book*, 1952, Musical Appendix Nos. 3–5.

27 John Ward: 'Spanish Musicians in Sixteenth-Century England', *Essays in Musicology in Honour of Dragan Plamenac on his 70th Birthday*, 1969, fn. 27, p. 363.

28 Bibliothèque du Conservatoire Royale, Brussels, MS 24.135.

29 Ward: *The Vihuela de Mano*, p. 186.

Chapter Three (pp. 41–61)

1 Don Sebastian de Covarrubias Orozco: *Tesoro de la Lengua Castellana, o Española.* 1611, entry 'vihuela'.

2 *rasgueado* (cf. Bermudo's term *música golpeado*) – strumming a succession of chords as opposed to plucking selected notes – *punteado*.

3 on the dating of this work see Emilio Pujol: 'Significación de Joan Carlos Amat (1572–1642) en la historia de la guitarra', *Anuario Musical*, vol. V, 1950.

4 Richard Hudson: 'The Concept of Mode in Italian Guitar Music during the first half of the 17th Century', *Acta Musicologica*, vol. XLII, 1970, p. 164.

5 Nigel Fortune: 'Giustiniani on Instruments', *Galpin Society Journal*, vol. V, 1952.

6 Nigel Fortune: *Italian secular song from 1600 to 1635*, 1953, p. 136.

7 e.g. Remigio Romano: *Prima (2a., 3a., 4a., e residuo) reccolta di bellisime canzonette*, 1625.

8 Further details on this technique are given by Sylvia Murphy: 'Seventeenth - Century Guitar Music: Notes on Rasgueado Performance', *Galpin Society Journal*, vol. XXI, 1968.

9 *Intavolatura facile*, 1620.

10 *Intavolatura di Chitarra Spagnuola*, Bk. 4, 2nd impression, Rome, 1627.

11 *op. cit.*, p. 181; analyses of early seventeenth - century guitar forms can be found in 'The *Zarabanda* and *Zarabanda Francese* in Italian Guitar Music of the Early 17th Century', *Musica Disciplina* XXIV, 1970, and 'The *Folia* Dance and the *Folia* Formula in 17th Century Guitar Music', *Musica Disciplina* XXV, 1971 by the same author; see also Thomas Walker: 'Ciaccona and Passacaglia: Remarks on their Origin and Early History', *Journal of the American Musicological Society* XXI, 3, 1968 and Richard Hudson: 'Further Remarks on the Passacaglia and Ciaconna', *Journal of the American Musicological Society*, vol. XXIII, 2, 1970.

12 Transcribed by Anton Stingl: *Neun Suiten*, Musikverlag Friedrich Hofmeister, Hofheim am Taunus.

13 On Briceño – François Lesure: 'Trois instrumentalistes françaises au XVIIe. siècle', *Revue de Musicologie*, 1955, p. 186; José Castro Escudero and Daniel Devoto: 'La méthode pour la guitare de Luis Briceño', *Revue de Musicologie*, Vol. LI, No. 2, 1965; Hélène Charnassé: 'A propos d'un récent article sur la méthode pour la guitare de Luis Briceño', *Revue de Musicologie*, vol. LII No. 2, 1966.

14 *op. cit.* 'To explain … the guitar'.

15 François Lesure: 'Le Traité des Instruments de Pierre Trichet', *Annales Musicologiques*, vol. IV, 1956, pp. 216–217.

16 references in Albert Cohen: 'A Study of Instrumental Ensemble Practice in Seventeenth-Century France', *Galpin Society Journal*, vol. XV, 1962.

17 Recent studies of Corbetta's music and the social background are 'The Guitar Cult in the Courts of Louis XIV and Charles II', *Guitar Review* 26, 1962, and '"La Guitare Royale": A study of the Career and Compositions of Francesco Corbetta', *Recherches sur la Musique Française Classique*, vol. VI, 1966, both by Richard Keith.

18 *The Term Catalogues: 1688–1709*, 1903, ed. Edward Arber; entry under Michaelmas Term 1677.

19 quoted by Keith, 'La Guitare Royale', p. 82.

20 quoted by Keith, 'La Guitare Royale', p. 80.

21 An isolated reference to the guitar's earlier presence in England comes from the accounts of the Earls of Rutland, in which an entry for April 1643 runs: Item paid to the 'gittarman' that taught the Lady Francis for two months, and for her book £4. 2. 6. Item paid the 'gittarman' for mending an instrument for my Lady Francis 7s., Walter L. Woodfill, op. cit., p. 272.

22 quoted by Michael Tilmouth: 'Some Improvements in Music noted by William Turner in 1697', *Galpin Society Journal*, vol. X, 1957.

23 *Roger North on Music*, ed. John Wilson, 1959, p. 307.

24 Michael Tilmouth: 'Nicola Matteis', *The Musical Quarterly*, January 1960.

25 Jeffrey Pulver: *Dictionary of Old English Music and Musical Instruments*, 1923.

26 Thurston Dart: 'The Cittern and its English Music', *Galpin Society Journal*, vol. I, 1948.

27 R. W. Strizich (ed.): *Robert de Visée, Oeuvres complètes pour guitare*, 1969, p. iv.

28 François Campion: *Vingt Pièces*, transcribed by Louis Baille, Editions Salabert, Paris, n.d.

29 *Instrucción*, p. 1.

30 The fact that neither Corbetta nor de Visée gives precise instructions about the tuning of the fifth course strings has led to a divergence of views; musical considerations have inclined Keith to favour the tuning aa dd' gg bb e'e' ('La Guitare Royale', p. 86) and Charnassé to prefer Aa dd' gg bb e' ('Sur l'accord de la Guitare', pp. 33–34). A useful survey of tunings has been compiled by Sylvia Murphy, 'The Tuning of the Five-course Guitar', *Galpin Society Journal*, vol. XXIII, 1970.

31 'La Guitare Royale', p. 88.

32 Van der Straeten, *op. cit.*, vol. VIII, p. 432, and Johannes Wolf, *op. cit.*, p. 218.

33 Ernst Pohlmann: *Laute, Theorbe, Chitarrone*, Bremen, 1968.

34 *Syntagma Musicum, Vol. 2, De Organographia*, 1619, p. 53.

35 *Musica Instrumentalis Deudsch, (1528)* reprint, 1896, p. 65.

36 Eugen Schmitz: 'Guitarrentabulaturen', *Monatshefte für Musikgeschichte*, vol. XXV, 1903, p. 137.

37 Hellmut Federhofer: 'Eine Angelica– und Gitarrentabulatur aus der zweiter Hälfte des 17. Jahrhunderts', *Festschrift für Walter Wiora*, Kassel, 1967; this collection has been partly transcribed by Hans Radke: 'Ausgewählte Stücke aus einer Angelica– und Gitarrentabulatur der 2. Hälfte des 17. Jahrhunderts, *Musik alter Meister*, 17, Graz, 1967.

38 MS. M.2209, Biblioteca Nacional, Madrid.

39 *Biblioteca nueva de los escritores aragoneses que florecieron desde el año 1689 hasta el de 1753*, vol. IV, 1800, pp. 224–5.

40 Rafael Mitjana: *La Musique en Espagne*, p. 2096.

41 Gaspar Sanz: *Instrucción*, facsimile ed., Prólogo y Notas de Luis García-Abrines, 2nd. ed. 1966, p. xivf.

42 Helene Wesseley-Kropik: *Lelio Colista*, 1961, p. 64f.

43 Partly transcribed by Josef Klima: 'Ausgewählte Werke der Auseer Gitarretabulatur des 18. Jahrhunderts', *Musik alter Meister*, 10, Graz, 1958; *Schmiticourante* pp. 3–4.

44 A number of German sources can be found in Wolf, *op. cit.*

45 *Histoire de la Musique*, 1743 ed., vol. I, p. 320.

46 Vol. VII, 1757.

47 It can also be seen in music from the transitional period, such as the guitar accompaniment to a song by the French guitarist Charles Doisy (reproduced in *Guitar Review* 35, 1971, pp. 28–29); the accompaniment was meant for a five-course guitar, but allowance was made for its performance on the six-string instrument by indicating the notes that could be played an octave lower.

48 Thomas Heck has described the

various stages of the development of notation in Chapter III of *The Birth of the Classic Guitar*, 1970; see also 'The role of Italy in the early history of the classic guitar', *Guitar Review* 34, 1971, by the same author.

Chapter Four (pp. 62–81)

1 *op. cit.*, p. 9.

2 George Hogarth: 'Musical Instruments: The Harp and Guitar', *The Musical World*, vol. III, No. XXXII, 1836, p. 85; this tuning is given by Fernando Ferrandiere, *Arte de tocar la Guitarra Española*, Madrid, 1799, quoted by Emilio Pujol, *Escuela Razonada de la Guitarra*, Buenos Aires, 1956, Book One, p. 41.

3 quoted by Charnassé: 'Sur 'l'Accord de la Guitare', p. 36.

4 Stephen Bonner: *The Classic Image*, p. 61.

5 Anthony Baines: *Victoria and Albert Museum Catalogue of Musical Instruments*, II, pp. 57–58, where the head is described as a nineteenth-century replacement.

6 *The Structure and Preservation of the Violin*, transl. T. Fardely, London, 1833, p. 28.

7 In considering the extant dated instruments of this period, one must bear in mind that many five-course guitars were adapted to take six single strings in the nineteenth century. The role of

what appear to be original six-string guitars of an earlier date than those considered here is not yet clear; e.g. a guitar by Thomas Andreas Hulinzký, in the National Museum, Prague, seems to have been made to take six strings. Alexander Buchner, *Musical Instruments through the Ages*, London, 1964, fig. 202, gives the date 1754, which is repeated in *Guitar Review* 35, p. 19. Until a thorough critical evaluation is made of all the instruments, the tunings and the music of this period, the closing decades of the eighteenth century must be regarded as a more realistic time for the emergence of the six-string guitar with the modern interval pattern, as publications of music for such an instrument did not begin to appear in any great number until the turn of the century.

8 Baines: *European and American Musical Instruments*, p. 50.

9 Heck: *The Birth of the Classic Guitar*, p. 45.

10 Collection Vladimir Bobri; see *Guitar Review* 35, p. 21. The series 'A Gallery of Great Guitars' in this journal was an excellent opportunity to provide a wealth of information on early instruments. Unfortunately it allows little comparative study, as measurements are not consistently given and detailed descriptions of the various features of the instruments are lacking.

11 *Carl Claudius' Samling Af Gamle Musikinstrumenter*, Copenhagen, 1931, No. 172, illustrated p. 147.

12 Heck: *op. cit.*, p. 44.

13 Baines: *loc. cit.*

14 Bonner: *op. cit.*, pp. 32–33.

15 *op. cit.*, p. 40.

16 Benedid's name has been given as *Benedict* or *Benedit*, perhaps because of the flourish of the last letter, visible on the label of his guitar in Plate 34e. The spelling of his name as 'Benediz' in *The Giulianiad* (see quote on p. 69) implies that the final letter is 'd'.

17 see remark by Julian Bream in the discussion after the paper by Thomas Binkley: 'Le luth et sa technique', *Le Luth et sa Musique* ed. Jean Jacquot, Paris, 1958, p. 34.

18 Donald Gill: 'James Talbot's Manuscript', *Galpin Society Journal*, vol. xv, 1962.

19 Baines: *op. cit.*, p. 49.

20 taken from the harp, Baines, *op. cit.*, p. 50.

21 Luis-Heitor Corrêa de Azevedo: 'La guitare archaïque au Brésil', pp. 121–22.

22 No. 1, p. 56.

23 Terence Usher: 'The Spanish Guitar in the Nineteenth and Twentieth Centuries', *Galpin Society Journal*, vol. ix, 1956.

24 illustrated *Guitar Review* 28, 1965, p. 6; a commercial valuation of Lacote's guitars towards

the end of the nineteenth century puts the highest price on
instruments with this device:
'ordinary model with pegs–
100–125 francs, ordinary model
with machine head–125–150
francs, superior model with
méchanique fermée – 200 – 250
francs', Robert Fissore: *Les
Maîtres Luthiers*, entry *Lacote*.

25 Helga Haupt: *Wiener Instrumentenbauer*, 1960, p. 136.

26 Bonner: *op. cit.*, p. 21.

27 Robert Fissore: *La Lutherie*,
Pt. II, p. 86.

28 *The Great Exhibition: London
1851*, reprint, London, 1970,
p. 97.

29 *Hints to Guitar Players with a
description of the Tripodion*, London, n.d. p. 10, Cambridge University Library, Mus. 25.8.(4).

30 quoted in L. G. Johnson:
General T. Perronet Thompson,
1957, p. 139.

31 L. G. Johnson: *op. cit.*, p. 158.

32 Robert Fissore: *Les Maîtres
Luthiers*, p. xvi; in spite of the
fact that Spanish guitars were
not as well finished as French
guitars, the author praises them
for their 'unbelievable sonority'.

33 Domingo Prat: *Diccionario*, p.
391.

34 Andrés Segovia: 'Guitar Strings
before and after Albert Augustine', *Guitar Review* 17, 1955.

35 Gerald Hayes: 'Instruments and

Instrumental Notation', *The
New Oxford History of Music*,
vol. IV, p. 725.

36 George Clinton: 'José Romanillos, Luthier', *Guitar*, December, 1972, p. 23.

37. Bermudo: *op. cit.* f. 28v.

Chapter Five (pp. 82–107)

1 *Encyclyopédie Pittoresque de la
Musique*, vol. 1, Paris, 1835,
p. 164 and p. 126; quoted by
Thomas Heck, 'The Role of
Italy in the Early History of the
Classic Guitar', *Guitar Review*,
34, 1971, fn. 6.

2 Manuel Rocamora: *Fernando Sor*
p. 14; the present account of Sor
is also based on William Sasser:
*The Guitar Works of Fernando
Sor*, and the same author's 'In
Search of Sor', *Guitar Review* 26,
1962.

3 see Yves Gérard: *Thematic,
Bibliographical and Critical Cata-
logue of the Works of Luigi
Boccherini*, p. 493ff. and p. 594.

4 *I Classici Italiani della Musica*, 4,
Boccherini, ed. Pina Carmirelli,
Rome, 1962; Boccherini's sketch
is reproduced on p. vii.

5 Rocamora: *op. cit.*, p. 9 and p. 49.

6 Thomas Heck: 'Mauro Giuliani, birth and death dates confirmed, *Guitar Review* 37, 1972,
p. 15; this author's thesis, *The
Birth of the Classic Guitar*.

7 translated by Heck, *op. cit.*, p. 145.

8 Heck, *op. cit.*, p. 226.

9 Jeffrey Pulver: *Paganini*, p. 43.

10 Paganini's works are listed in Renée de Saussine: *Paganini*, pp. 259–261.

11 Pulver: *op. cit.*, p. 45.

12 *op. cit.* tr. Mary Cowden Clarke, n.d. p. 67.

13 *op. cit.*, pp. 69–70.

14 In spite of Schubert's liking for the guitar, the only authentic publication to involve the instrument is the *Kantata zur Namensfeier des Vaters*, for two tenors, bass voice and guitar (a (a simple arpeggio accompaniment). His 'Guitar Quartet' is the Notturno, Op. 21 by Wenzel Matiegka, to which Schubert added a 'cello part; see Otto Erich Deutsch: *Schubert: Die Dokumente seines Lebens*, p. 30.

15 British Museum shelf no. 9.668.a.

16 *The Sonata in the Classic Era*, p. 664.

17 *The Guitar Works*, p. 98.

18 Willi Apel: *Harvard Dictionary of Music*, 1966, p. 281, entry *Freistimmig*.

19 Sasser: *op. cit.*, p. 136.

20 Heck: *op. cit.*, p. 208ff. reports on the popularity of vocal as well as instrumental variations.

21 *op. cit.*, pp. 38–39, where it appears with simple Albertibass type accompaniments.

22 Sor's sole composition for guitar and strings was the *Sinfonia Concertante*, the score of which has not apparently survived; this was performed on 24 March 1817 in London, on the occasion when Sor, the only guitarist to do so, appeared at a Royal Philharmonic Concert.

23 Philip J. Bone states that *The Giulianiad* was edited by Ferdinand Pelzer, *The Guitar and Mandolin*, p. 140; there does not appear to be any evidence for this.

24 No. 1, Introduction, p. 2.

25 *op. cit.*, p. 3.

26 *op. cit.*, p. 10.

27 *op. cit.*, p. 11.

28 *op. cit.*, p. 27: It is difficult to understand why the 'guitar-quacks' should have 'prayed'; 'pray' is probably a mistake, as the phrase 'many who went to scoff, remained to praise' seems to have been part of the critics' jargon; it occurs in a review of a concert by Derwort in *The Musical World* 1, No. 12, p. 188.

29 *op. cit.*, p. 38.

30 *op. cit.*, p. 40.

31 *op. cit.*, p. 47.

32 *op. cit.*, p. 48.

33 *The Musical World* iii, No. 27, 1836, pp. 12–13.

34 quoted by Frank Mott Harrison: *Reminiscences of Mme. Sidney Pratten*, pp. 22–23.

35 Harrison: *op. cit.*, p. 58.

36 Cambridge University Library, Mus. 25, 8(9).

37 George Henry Derwort: *New Method of Learning the Spanish Guitar*, p. 7.

38 This is recommended by Nicario Jauralde: *A Complete Preceptor for the Spanish Guitar*, p. 5.

39 *op. cit.*, p. 6.

40 Mme. Pratten: *Guitar Tutor*, p. 7.

41 *loc. cit.*

42 *op. cit.*, p. 6.

43 *Hints to Guitar Players*, p. 9.

44 Duvernay: *op. cit.*, pp. 6–7.

45 *Instructions for the Spanish Guitar*, p. 2.

46 Cambridge University Library, Mus. 55, 19(16).

47 Vladimir Bobri has suggested the practice originated with Flamenco guitarists, who may have developed the technique to achieve greater volume when accompanying singing and dancing, *The Segovia Technique*, p. 44.

48 A discussion of its history can be found in Emilio Pujol: *The Dilemma of Timbre on the Guitar*, 1960; see also Adolf Koczirz: 'Uber die Fingernageltechnik bei Saiteninstrumenten', *Festschrift für Guido Adler*, 1930; advice on the care of the nails can be found in Malcolm Weller: 'Nails', *Guitar*, February, 1973.

49 *op. cit.*, pp. 8–9.

50 The programme from which the titles of the guitars solos are taken is pasted to the inside back cover of the copy of *Learning the Guitar Simplified by Mme. Pratten* in the University Library, Cambridge, shelf mark Mus. 2. 58(1).

51 Illustrated in Baines, *European and American Musical Instruments*, fig. 306.

52 Bruno Tonazzi: *Miguel Llobet*, p. 12.

Chapter Six (pp. 108–126)

1 Ralph Kirkpatrick: *Domenico Scarlatti*, p. 196.

2 J. B. Trend: *Manuel de Falla and Spanish Music*, p. 39.

3 *Manuel de Falla; His Life and Works*, pp. 112–113.

4 Bruno Tonazzi (*Miguel Llobet, Chitarrista dell' Impressionismo*, pp. 19–20) gives as the reason 'the technique is too complicated and one needs to know the instrument'; this information was related in a letter to Tonazzi by Mario Castelnuovo-Tedesco, who was repeating what Andrés Segovia had been told by Debussy's widow; Tonazzi finds this testimony 'very strange', as Llobet encouraged a number of modern composers to write for the guitar.

5 Pahissa: *op. cit.*, p. 110.

6 Bobri: *op. cit.*, p. 29.

7 Bobri: *op. cit.*, pp. 48–49; one can still come across conflicting advice: 'It is of the utmost importance that, if the nails are to be used, then the nail and *only* the nail should strike the string. A combined flesh and nail technique gives the worst of both, and the best of neither'. Hector Quine: *Introduction to the Guitar*, London, 1971, p. 4.

8 *Guitar Review*, 22, 1958.

9 Castelnuovo–Tedesco's complete guitar works have been listed by Ronald C. Purcell, 'Mario Castelnuovo-Tedesco and the Guitar', *Guitar Review* 27, 1972, pp. 3–4.

10 quoted by Martha Nelson: 'Canarios', *Guitar Review* 25, 1961.

11 A consideration of these problems can be found in Julian Bream: 'How to write for the guitar', *The Score*, 19, March 1957, and Isabel Smith: 'Performer's Platform – Letter from a Guitarist', *The Composer*, Autumn 1967.

12 'The Guitar – an Evaluation', *The Musical Times*, vol. xcv, November 1954, p. 597.

13 Margaret Campbell: 'Everybody's Instrument', *The Times Educational Supplement*, 24 May, 1968.

14 Graham Wade: 'The Guitar in Primary Education', *Making Music* No. 72, Spring 1970.

List of Plates

(*b*) Rear view of a five-course guitar by the same maker 1646; the back of this instrument is similar to that of the four-course guitar in (*a*). *Courtesy of the Sammlung alter Musikinstrumente, Kunsthistorisches Museum, Vienna.*

14 Front and rear views of the five-course guitar by Belchior Dias. *Courtesy of The Royal College of Music, London.*

15 Guitarist featured on the title page of *Vocabolari molt profitos per apendre Lo Catalan Alamany y lo Alamany Catalan*, (Perpinya, 1502) *Courtesy of the Biblioteca Central, Barcelona.*

16 (*a*) from Francisco Guerrero's *Sacrae Cantiones*, (Seville, 1555). *Courtesy of The Hispanic Society of America.* (*b*) Title page of Guillaume Morlaye's first book of pieces for four-course guitar. *Courtesy of the Vadianabibliothek, St. Gall.*

17 (*a*) French four-course guitarist; (*b*) Gaspar Duiffoprugcar (1514–1571), etching by Pierre Woeiriot, 1562. *Courtesy of the Bibliothèque Nationale, Paris.*

18 Quintern Player, one of a series of ten engravings attributed to Tobias Stimmer (1539–84). The verse accompanying the engraving has been translated: 'One obviously sees that the quintern was modelled after the fiedel. Just by the looks of the instrument we are guided to the conclusion that it served as an introduction to the lute, for accompanying song composition and reciting old tales. We must preserve this tradition of our elders'. *Courtesy of The New York Public Library, Astor, Lenox and Tilden Foundations.*

19 Drawing of a four-course guitar by Jacques Cellier, (B. N. Paris, Ms. Fr. 9152, f. 190, *c.* 1585). The intervals of the four courses are correctly described, but the tuning in notation is for a five-course instrument. *Courtesy of the Bibliothèque Nationale, Paris.*

20 Bronze casting by Peter Vischer the Younger (1487–1582) in the Church of St. Sebaldus, Nuremberg. *Courtesy of Bärenreiter-Bild-Archiv.*

21 (*a*) Front (*b*) side and (*c*) rear views of a guitar by René Voboam (*d*) Its sunken rose; the six-pointed star was a popular design and such roses appear on a number of early guitars. *Courtesy of The Ashmolean Museum, Oxford.*

22 (*a*) Two guitars in the collection of W. E. Hill & Sons, London. The one on the left (*b*) may be the work of Champion; the one on the right (*c*) is by Alexandre Voboam, dated 1652 (*d*). Both instruments have been converted for use as a six-string guitar.

23 (*a*) Front and (*b*) rear views of a chitarra battente by Jacobus Stadler. (*c*) Detail of the hunting scene on the side. (*d*) Five-course chitarra battente by unknown maker with three strings to each course. *Courtesy of W. E. Hill & Sons, London.*

24 (*a*) Front and (*b*) rear views of

a six-course guitar by Joachim Tielke. Tielke's excellent workmanship is visible in the detailed views of the head (*c*) and the inlaid scene on the side (*d*). *Courtesy of The Victoria and Albert Museum.* (*e*) Five-course guitar by Tielke. *Courtesy of The Royal College of Music, London.*

25 Rear view of a guitar by Matteo Sellas. *Courtesy of The Victoria and Albert Museum, London.*

26 (*a*) Front, (*b*) side and (*c*) rear views of a chitarra battente by Giorgo Sellas. *Courtesy of the Ashmolean Museum, Oxford.* (*d*) Neck by Giorgio Sellas. *Courtesy of the Victoria and Albert Museum, London.* (*e*) Rear and (*f*) Front views of a guitar which may be the work of Sellas; this instrument has been converted to take six strings, a common nineteenth - century practice. *Courtesy of the Syndics of the Fitzwilliam Museum, Cambridge.*

27 (*a*) Front, (*b*) side and (*c*) rear views of a five-course guitar by Antonio Stradivarius, 1688(?) *Courtesy of the Ashmolean Museum Oxford.*

28 (*a*) Front and (*b*) rear views of the so-called Rizzio guitar. (*c*) From left to right: guitar of South German or Italian make, French guitar, attributed to one of the Voboams, the 'Rizzio' guitar and the guitar by Belchior Dias. The size of the 'Rizzio' guitar is closer to that of the two seventeenth-century guitars on the left than to that of the sixteenth-century instrument. *Cour-*

tesy of The Royal College of Music, London.

29 Joos van Craesbeeck's painting is a rare instance of an illustration of a four-course guitarist playing from tablature. The painting is in Dessau Castle. *Courtesy of Bildarchiv Foto Marburg.*

30 Sixteenth-century vihuela and four-course guitar tablatures: (*a*) Milán's sixth pavane, from *El Maestro* (1536); (*b*) Narváez's *Guárdame las vacas* theme, from *Los Seys Libros del Delphin* (*1538*). In Milan's tablature, the top line represents the top string, which in the tablatures of the other vihuelistas is represented by the bottom line, as in (*b*). (*c*) from Melchiore de Barberiis' *Contina* (1549); (*d*) from Fuenllana's *Orphenica Lyra* (1554); (*e*) from Gregoire Brayssing's *Quart Livre* (1553). In the Italian (*c*) and French (*e*) examples, the top line represents the highest string, while Fuenllana follows the general vihuela practice of indicating this by the bottom line of the tablature. (There are a number of misprints in Barberiis' *Fantasia*: bar 3, 0 on third line should be 2; bar 4, 3 should be on the second line; bar 5, 5 should be 0; bar 8, second 3 should be 2; bar 10, 3 on the top line should be 2.) *Courtesy of the Trustees of the British Museum.*

31 Seventeenth-century tablatures: (*a*) Amat's chord table. (*b*) *Romanesca* from Benedetto

Sanseverino's *Intavolatura Facile* (1620); the letters refer to the chord alphabet given at the beginning of the book, the values of the rasgueado strokes being shown by the notes above the line. (*c*) *Gagliarda* from Foscarini's *Il Primo, Secondo e Terzo Libro* (*c. 1629*); the alphabet chords are still used, but a more interesting texture is achieved by the addition of written out notes. (*d*) from Corbetta's *La Guitarre Royalle* (1671); the alphabet system has been abandoned, all the notes being indicated by letters. The King who liked this gigue was Charles II. (*e*) The beginning of the transition from tablature to modern notation appears in *Les Dons d'Apollon* by Michel Corrette (1763). *Courtesy of the Trustees of the British Museum.*

32 Portrait of Corbetta; from *Varii Scherzi di Sonate per la Chitara Spagnola*, Brussels, 1648. *Courtesy of the Trustees of the British Museum.*

33 Title page of Remy Médard's *Pièces de Guitarre* (1676). The foot-stool appears to be more decorative than functional, as the guitar is not resting on the left leg; the many early illustrations of guitarists generally show the performer, if seated, supporting the instrument on crossed legs.

34 Studies of a guitarist by Jean-Antoine Watteau. The guitar appears in many of Watteau's paintings, and in these two studies he demonstrates his keen eye for detail in distinguishing the two right-hand positions described in Diderot and d'Alembert's *Encyclopédie*. *Courtesy of the Trustees of the British Museum.*

35 (*a*) Front, (*b*) side and (*c*) rear views of a six-course guitar by José Benedid (end of the eighteenth century), one of the earliest guitars with fan-strutting, visible in (*d*), which shows details of the internal construction of the instrument. (*e*) The Benedid label; note the paper lining, a common practice in early instrument making; in this case sheets of music have been used. *Courtesy of Jack and Dorinda Schuman.*

36 (*a*) Front and (*b*) rear view of a six-string guitar by Giovanni Battista Fabricatore, Naples, 1798. *Courtesy of Jack and Dorinda Schuman.* (*c*) Recessed fingerboard; the label of this guitar reads: *Gennaro Fabricatore Anno 1822 Napoli Strada S. Giacomo No. 42.* Note the rectangular shape of the frets. *Courtesy of Tony Bingham.*

37 (*a*) The excessive waisting is a feature of the north European nineteenth-century guitar. This instrument has the maker's name – WEISSGERBER – stamped on the inside of the back. (*b*) Its fingerboard has the frets level with the surface of the wood, which enables the fingers to slide more easily than when

the frets are raised. *Courtesy of Tony Bingham.*

38 (*a*) Front and (*b*) rear views of a guitar by Louis Pontormo, 1833. *Courtesy of Tony Bingham.* (*c*) Front and (*d*) rear views of a guitar by Josef Pages, 1809. *Courtesy of the Royal College of Music, London.*

39 Types of bridges: (*a*) on the Belchior Dias guitar; (*b*) on the so-called Rizzio guitar – designed to take six strings, so presumably a later addition. *Courtesy of the Royal College of Music, London.* (*c*) on a five-course guitar in the collection of W. E. Hill & Sons, London; (*d*) pin-bridge on a guitar by René François Lacote; (*e*) modern bridge from the José Ramirez guitar (*see Plate 45*).

40 (*a*) Front and (*b*) rear views of a guitar by Rafael Vallejo. *Courtesy of the Victoria and Albert Museum, London.*

41 The Guitarpa, invented by José Gallegos. After the Catalogue of the Great Exhibition of 1851.

42 The Enharmonic Guitar, designed by General Thompson, from Plate ii, frontispiece of *Instructions to my Daughter. Courtesy of the Trustees of the British Museum.*

43 (*a*) Guitar by José Pernas (1843) and (*b*) guitar by Torres (1888); these two instruments well illustrate the transition from the early nineteenth-century guitar to the modern instrument. *Formerly Winkler Collection.*

44 (*a*) Signed portrait of Catharina Josepha Pratten, dated 1853; 'It is advisable that when any of the three fingers are used without the thumb, the thumb should rest on one of the silver strings, and also, if the thumb alone is striking a succession of notes on the silver strings, the three fingers should rest on the gut strings, as shown in the frontispiece.' (*Guitar Tutor,* 1881, p. 7). (*b*) Drawings of the right hand from Mme. Pratten's *Learning the Guitar Simplified,* 10th ed., 1893. The positions of the hands contrasts sharply with those of the modern guitarist (cf. *Plate 46 (e)* and *(f). Courtesy of the Trustees of the British Museum.* (*c*) The label of this guitar reads: *Model of guitar as used by Mme. Sidney Pratten and their Royal Highnesses the Princess Louise and the Princess Beatrice,* London, 1881; excessively decorated guitars such as these were the result of the nineteenth-century dilettante approach to the instrument. *Courtesy of the Spanish Guitar Centre, Bristol.* (*d*) *The Bambina,* an octave guitar introduced by Mme. Pratten. *Courtesy of Jack and Dorinda Schuman.*

45 (*a*) A modern guitar alongside the sixteenth century guitar by Belchior Dias and the seventeenth century guitar in the Fitzwilliam Museum, Cambridge illustrate the extent of the physical growth of the instrument. Modern decoration

is limited to an inlaid motif round the soundhole (*b*), which is sometimes repeated on the bridge. The mosaic pattern is made of strips of different coloured woods, glued together to form a 'log', slices of which are placed alongside each other (*c*). The modern guitar is from the workshops of José Ramirez.

46 Nineteenth- and Twentieth-Century Guitarists: (*a*) and (*b*) Title pages of two of the guitar tutors published in England in the early nineteenth century; (*c*) from Marziano Bruni's *Treatise on the Guitar*; (*d*) from Flamini Duvernay's *Complete Instruction Book for the Guitar*; (*e*) drawing of Miguel Llobet by Charles Léandre (from *Mercure Musicale*, No. 2, 1906). (*f*) Julian Bream and John Williams.

The early nineteenth-century guitarists (*a, b, c, d,*) held the instrument in various ways; on the right leg, on the left and generally with a ribbon. Not until the second half of the century did the modern approach to the instrument become standard (*e*). Looking at the right hand, as Llobet is

doing, is necessary in the production of artificial harmonics; otherwise the guitarist watches his left hand to ensure accurate stopping down in changes along the fingerboard. The positioning of the hands of the classical guitarist, a most important aspect of technique, is well illustrated in the side view of Williams; the right hand adopts a high position to allow the thumb and fingers complete freedom of attack, while the left hand is turned to give well-balanced support to all the fingers. (*a*), (*b*), (*c*), (*d*) and (*e*) *Courtesy of the Trustees of the British Museum*, (*f*) *Courtesy of the 'Radio Times'*.

47 David Rubio assembling a guitar in his workshop in Duns Tew. The Spanish method of attaching the neck to the body can clearly be seen; the sides are fitted into slots in the heel, and, when the table and back are fitted, an extremely strong joint is achieved. In the dovetail method the body is completely asembled before the neck is attached. *Author's photograph.*

Bibliography

MUSIC SOURCES

Vihuela

Daza, Esteban: *Libro de Música en cifras para Vihuela, intitulado El Parnaso*, Valladolid, 1576.

Fuenllana, Miguel de: *Libro de Música para Vihuela, intitulado Orphenica Lyra*, Sevilla, 1554.

Milán, Luis: *Libro de Música de Vihuela de Mano, intitulado El Maestro*, Valencia, 1536; modern edition – Jacobs, Charles: *El Maestro*, Pennsylvania and London, 1971.

Mudarra, Alonso: *Tres Libros de música en cifra para vihuela*, Sevilla, 1546; modern edition – Pujol, Emilio: *Monumentos de la Música Española*, VII, Barcelona, 1949.

Narvaez, Luys de: *Los Seys Libros del Delphin de Música de Cifra para tañer vihuela*, Valladolid, 1538; modern edition – Pujol, Emilio: *Monumentos de la Música Española*, III, Barcelona, 1945.

Pisador, Diego: *Libro de Música de Vihuela, agora nuevamente combuesto*, Salamanca, 1552.

Valderrábano, Enríquez de: *Libro de música de vihuela, intitulado Silva de Sirenas*, Valladolid, 1547; modern edition – Pujol, Emilio: *Monumentos de la Música Española*, XXII and XXIII, Barcelona, 1965.

Four-course Guitar

Barberiis, Melchiore de: *Opera intitolata Contina, intabolatura di lauto di fantasie, motetti, canzoni, discordate a varii modi. Fantasie per sonar uno solo con uno Lauti & farsi tenore & soprano: Madrigali per sonar a dui Lauti: Fantasie per sonar sopra la Chitara da sette corde*, Venice, 1549.

Brayssing, Grégoire: *Quart Livre de Tabulature de Guiterre, contenant plusieurs Fantasies, Pseaulmes, & Chansons, avec L'Alouette, & La Guerre*, Paris, 1553.

Fuenllana, Miguel de: see under Vihuela.

Gorlier, Simon: *Le Troysieme Livre contenant plusieurs Duos, et Trios, avec la Bataille de Janequin a trois, nouvellement mis en tabulature de*

Guiterne, par Simon Gorlier, excellent joueur, Paris, 1551.

Le Roy, Adrien: *Premier Livre de Tabulature de Guiterre, contenant plusieurs Chansons, Fantaisies, Pavanes, Gaillardes, Almandes, Branles, tant simple qu'autres*, Paris, 1551.

—— *Tiers Livre de Tabulature de Guiterre, contenant plusieurs Preludes, Basse-dances, Tourdions, Pavanes, Gaillardes, Almandes, Bransles, tant doubles que simples*, Paris, 1552.

—— *Cinquiesme Livre de Guiterre, contenant plusieurs Chansons a trois & quatre parties, par bons & excelens Musiciens*, Paris 1555.

—— *Second Livre de Guiterre, contenant plusieurs Chansons en forme de Voix de Ville*, Paris, 1555.

Morlaye, Guillaume: *Le Premier Livre de Chansons, Gaillardes, Pavannes, Bransles, Almandes, Fantaisies, reduict en tabulature de Guiterne*, Paris, 1552.

—— *Quatriesme Livre contenant plusieurs Fantaisies, Chansons, Gaillardes, Paduanes, Bransles, reduictes en tabulature de Guyterne*, Paris, 1552.

—— *Le Second Livre de Chansons, Gaillardes, Paduanes, Bransles, Almandes, Fantasies, reduict en tabulature de Guiterne*, Paris, 1553.

Mudarra, Alonso: see under *Vihuela*.

Phalèse, Pierre: *Selectissima elegantissimaque, Gallica, Italica et Latina in Guiterna ludenda carmina, quibus adduntur & Fantasie, Passomezzi, Salterelli, Galliardi, Almandes, Branles & similia, ex optima elegantissimaque collecta, & iam cum omni diligentia recens impressa. His abcessit luculenta quaedem & perutilis Institutio qua quisque citra alicuius subsidium artem facillime percipiet*, Louvain and Antwerp, 1570.

Five-course Guitar

The following is by no means a complete list of publications for the five-course guitar in the seventeenth and eighteenth centuries; further references can be found in Wolf, Johannes: *Handbuch der Notationskunde* Vol. II, Leipzig, 1919, and in Boetticher, Wolfgang: 'Gitarrenmusik', *Die Musik in Geschichte und Gegenwart*, vol. v, cols. 180–202.

Amat, Juan Carlos: *Guitarra Española de cinco órdenes*, Gerona, 1639.

An, Princes: *Princes An's Lute Book*, MS., n.d.

Briceño, Luis de: *Método mui facilissimo para aprender a tañer la guitarra a lo Español*, Paris, 1626; facsimile edition, Minkoff Reprint, Geneva, 1972.

Calvi, Carlo: *Intavolatura di Chitarra e Chitarriglia*, Bologna, 1646.

Campion, François: *Nouvelles Découvertes sur la Guitare*, Paris, 1705.

Cocq, François le: *Recueil de pièces de guitarre*, 1729.

Colonna, Giovanni Ambrosio: *Intavolatura di Chitarra Spagnuola del primo, secondo, terzo, et quarto Libro*, Milan, 1637.

Corbetta, Francesco: *Scherzi Armonici trovati e facilitati in alcune curiosissime Suonate sopra la Chitarra Spagnuola*, Bologna, 1639.
—— *Varii Capricci per la Ghittara Spagnuola*, Milan, 1643.
—— *Varii Scherzi di Sonate per la Chitara Spagnola*, Brussels, 1648.
—— *La Guitarre Royalle*, Paris, 1671 and 1674.
Corrette, Michel: *Les Dons d'Apollon: Méthode pour apprendre facilement à jouer de la Guitarre*, Paris, 1763.

Foscarini, Giovanni Paolo: *Il primo, secõdo e terzo libro della Chitarra Spagnola*, c. 1629.

Granata, Giovanni Battista: *Capricci Armonici sopra la Chittariglia Spagnola*, Bologna, 1646.
—— *Armoniosi Toni di varie Suonate Musicali per la Chitarra Spagnuola et altre Suonate concertate a doi Violini e Basso*, Op. 7, Bologna, 1648 edition.
Guerau, Don Francisco: *Poema Harmonico compuesto de varias cifras por el temple de la Guitarra Española*, Madrid, 1694.

Kremberg, Jacob: *Musikalischen Gemüths-Ergötzung*, Dresden, 1689.

Majer, Joseph Friedrich Bernhardt Caspar: *Neu-eröffneter Theoretischer und Praktischer Music Saal*, Nuremberg, 1741.
Matteis, Nicola: *The false consonances of musick or Instructions for the playing of a true Base upon the Guitarre*, London, 1682.

Médard, Remy: *Pièces de Guitare*, Paris, 1676.

Montesardo, Girolomo: *Nuova Inventione d'Intavolatura per sonare li balleti sopra la Chitarra Spagnuola, senza numeri e note*, Florence, 1606.
Murcia, Santiago de: *Resumen de Acompanar la Parte con la Guitarra*, 1714.

Pellegrini, Domenico: *Armoniosi concerti sopra la chitarra spagnuola*, Bologna, 1650.

Ribayez, Don Lucas Ruiz de: *Luz y norte musical para caminar por las cifras de la Guitarra Española, y Arpa, tañer, y cantar a compás por canto de Organo*, Madrid, 1677.
Romano, Remigio: *Prima (secunda, terza, quarta) Raccolta di bellissime canzonette musicali*, Pavia, 1625.
Roncalli, Ludovico: *Capricci Armonici sopra la Chitarra Spagnola*, Bergamo, 1692.

Sanseverino, Benedetto: *Intavolatura facile*, Milan, 1620.
Sanz, Gaspar: *Instrucción de Música sobre la Guitarra Española*, Saragossa, 1674, facsimile edition, Prologue and Notes by Luis Garcia-Abrines, Institucion 'Fernando el Catolico', Saragossa, 1966.
Sotos, Andrés de: *Arte para aprender con facilidad y sin maestro la guitarra de cinco órdenes*, Madrid, 1764.

Velasco, Nicolas Doizi de: *Nuevo Modo de Cifra para tañer la Guitarra*, Naples, 1640.
Visée, Robert de: *Livre de Guittarre dédié au Roy*, Paris, 1682.
—— *Livre de Pièces pour la Guitarre*, Paris, 1686; modern edition – Strizich, Robert W.: *Oeuvres com-*

plètes pour guitare, Le Pupitre No. 15, Collection de Musique Ancienne publiée sous la Direction de François Lesure, Paris, 1969.

Six-string Guitar

It is impossible in the space of a bibliography to give more than the merest outline of publications of methods and music for the guitar in the nineteenth and twentieth centuries. References to a number of works can be found in P. J. Bone, *The Guitar and Mandolin*, London, 1954, *passim*, but caution is necessary in consulting this source; Sor's works have been listed by William Sasser, 'In Search of Sor', *Guitar Review*, No. 26, 1962, pp. 20–21, and *The Guitar Works of Fernando Sor*, Ph.D. dissertation, University of North Carolina, 1960, Chapter IV; an excellent source for Giuliani is Thomas Heck's *Thematic Catalogue of the Complete Works of Mauro Giuliani*, vol. II of his Ph.D. dissertation, *The Birth of the Classic Guitar*, Yale University, 1970; Tárrega's works appear in Emilio Pujol, *Tárrega*, Lisbon, 1960, pp. 259–266; Llobet's compositions and transcriptions can be found in Bruno Tonazzi's *Miguel Llobet, Chitarrista dell' Impressionismo*, Ancona and Milan, 1966, pp. 43–46.

Books and Articles

Agricola, Martin: *Musica Instrumentalis Deudsch*, Wittemberg, 1528 and 1545, reprint Leipzig, 1896.

Anglés, Higinio: 'Latin Church Music on the Continent 3 – Spain and Portugal', *The New Oxford History of Music*, vol. IV, Oxford, 1968.

Apel, Willi: 'Early Spanish Music for Lute and Keyboard Instruments', *Musical Quarterly*, XX, 1934.

—— *The Notation of Polyphonic Music 900–1600*, 5th ed., Cambridge, Mass., 1953.

—— 'Solo Instrumental Music', *The New Oxford History of Music*, vol. IV, Oxford, 1968.

Arbeau, Thoinot: *Orchesography* (1588), tr. Cyril W. Beaumont, with preface by Peter Warlock, London, 1925.

Arber, Edward: *The Term Catalogues, 1688–1709. A Contemporary Bibliography of English Literature in the reigns of Charles II, James II, William and Mary and Anne*, 3 vols., London, 1903–6.

Baines, Anthony: (ed.) *Musical Instruments through the Ages*, Harmondsworth, 1961.

—— *European and American Musical Instruments*, London, 1966.

—— *Victoria and Albert Museum Catalogue of Musical Instruments*, vol. II, Non-Keyboard Instruments, London, 1968.

Bal, J.: 'Fuenllana and the Transcription of Spanish Lute (Vihuela) Music', *Acta Musicologica* XI, 1939.

Baldini, Ugo: *Note di Tecnologia construttiva su la Chitarra*, 2nd. ed., Modena and Milan, 1957.

Barber, J. Murray: *Tuning and Temperament. A Historical Survey*, Michigan, 1953.

Bellow, Alexander, *The Illustrated History of the Guitar*, New York, 1970.

Berlioz, Hector: *A Treatise on Modern Instrumentation and Orchestration*, tr. Mary Cowden Clarke, London, n.d.

Bermudo, Juan: *Declaración de instrumentos musicales*, 1555; facsimile edition, *Documenta Musicologica* XI, Kassel, 1957.

Berner, A, van der Meer, J. H., Thibault, G. with the collaboration of Norman Brommelle: *Preservation and Restoration of Musical Instruments*, London, 1967

Bessaraboff, Nicholas: *Ancient European Musical Instruments, An Organological Study of the Musical Instruments in the Leslie Lindsey Mason Collection at the Museum of Fine Arts, Boston*, New York, 1941.

Binkley, Thomas E.: 'Le Luth et sa Technique', *Le Luth et sa Musique*, ed. Jean Jacquot, Paris 1958.

Bobri, Vladimir: *The Segovia Technique*, New York, 1972.

Bone, Philip James: *The Guitar and Mandolin*, 2nd. ed., London, 1954.

—— 'Paganini and the Guitar', *Hinrichsen's Musical Year Book*, vol. VII, London, 1952.

Bonner, Stephen: *The Classic Image*, Harlow, 1972.

Boyden, David D.: *Catalogue of The Hill Collection of Instruments in the Ashmolean Museum, Oxford*, Oxford, 1969.

Bream, Julian: 'How to write for the guitar', *The Score*, No. 19, March, 1957.

Brenan, Gerald: *The Literature of the Spanish People*, Harmondsworth, 1963.

Brondi, Maria Rita: 'Il liuto e la chitarra', *Rivista Musicale Italiana*, vol. XXXII, 1925, and vol. XXXIII, 1926.

—— *Il liuto e la chitarra*, Torino, 1926.

Brown, Howard Mayer: *Instrumental Music printed before 1600. A Bibliography*, Harvard, 1965.

Bruni, Antonio Bartholomeo: *Un Inventaire sous la Terreur. État des instruments de musique relevés chez les emigrés et condamnés*, Introduction, notices biographiques et notes par J. Gallay, Paris, 1890.

Buchner, Alexander: *Musical Instruments through the Ages*, London, 1961.

Buek, Fritz: *Die Gitarre und ihre Meister*, 4th. ed., Berlin, 1926.

Campbell, Margaret: 'Everybody's Instrument', *The Times Educational Supplement*, May 24, 1968.

Carfagna, Carlo and Caprani, Alberto: *Profilo Storico della Chitarra*, Ancona and Milan, 1966.

—— and Gangi, Mario: *Dizionario Chitarristico Italiano*, Ancona,1968

Cellini, Benvenuto: *Autobiography*, tr. George Bull, Harmondsworth, 1956.

Charnassé, Hélène: 'La Guitare', *Connaissance des Arts*, November, 1965.

—— 'A propos d'un récent article sur la méthode pour la guitare de Luis Briceño', *Revue de Musicologie*, vol. LII, No. 2, 1966.

—— 'Sur l'Accord de la Guitare',

Recherches sur la Musique Française Classique, vol. VII, 1967.

Chase, Gilbert: *The Music of Spain*, 2nd. revised ed., New York, 1959.

Chilesotti, Oscar: 'Notes sur le guitariste Robert de Visée', *Sammelbänder der Internationalen Musikgesellschaft*, vol. IX, 1907–8.

Chouquet, Gustave: *Le Musée du Conservatoire nationale de Musique. Catalogue raisonné des instruments de cette collection*, Supplements by L. Pillaut, Paris 1894–1903.

Clemencic, René: *Old Musical Instruments*, London, 1968.

Clinton, George: 'David Rubio, Master Craftsman', *Guitar*, vol. I, No. 3, October, 1972.

—— 'José Romanillos, Luthier', *Guitar*, vol. I, No. 5, December, 1972.

—— 'Robert Bouchet: Luthier', *Guitar*, vol. I, No. 7, February, 1973.

Cohen, Albert: 'A Study of Instrumental Ensemble Practice in Seventeenth - Century France', *Galpin Society Journal*, vol. XV, 1962.

Corrêa de Azevedo, Luis-Heitor: 'La guitare archaïque au Brésil', *Studia Memoriae Belae Bartok Sacra*, Budapest, 1956.

Coutagne, Henri: *Gaspard Duiffoproucart et les Luthiers lyonnais du XVIe. siècle*, Paris, 1893.

Dart, R. Thurston: 'The Cittern and its English Music', *Galpin Society Journal*, vol. I, 1948.

—— 'Instruments in the Ashmolean Museum', *Galpin Society Journal*, vol. VII, 1948.

Denis, Valentin: *De Muziekinstrumenten in de Nederlanden en in Italië naar hun Afbeelding in de 15e-eeuwsche Kunst*, Louvain, 1944.

Deutsch, Erich Otto: *Schubert; Die Dokumente seines Lebens*, Leipzig, 1964.

Devoto, Daniel: 'Métamorphoses d'une cithare', *Revue de Musicologie*, vol. XLI, July, 1958.

—— 'Poésie et musique dans l'oeuvre des Vihuelistes', *Annales Musicologiques*, IV, 1956.

Diderot, Denis and d'Alembert, Jean le Rond: *Encyclopédie, ou Dictionnaire raisonné des sciences, des arts et des métiers*, Paris, 1751–65.

Dolmetsch, Nathalie: *The Viola da Gamba, its Origin and History, its Technique and Musical Resources*, London, 1962.

Emmerson, F. G.: *Tudor Secretary: Sir William Petre at Court and Home*, Cambridge, Mass., 1961.

Escudero, José Castro: 'La Méthode pour la Guitare de Luis Briceño, *Revue de Musicologie*, vol. LI, No. 2, 1965.

Engel, Carl: *A Descriptive Catalogue of the Musical Instruments in the South Kensington Museum*, 2nd. ed., London, 1874.

Federhofer, Hellmut: 'Eine Angelica- und Gitarrentabulatur aus der zweiten Hälfte des 17. Jahrhunderts', *Festschrift für Walter Wiora*, Kassel, 1967.

Fissore, Robert: *Les Maîtres Luthiers*, 4th. ed., Paris, *c.* 1890.

—— *La Lutherie*, Pts. I and II, Paris, 1900.

Fortune, Nigel: 'Giustiniani on Instruments', *Galpin Society Journal*, vol. V, 1952.

—— *Italian Secular Song from 1600 to 1635*, unpublished Ph.D. thesis, Cambridge University, 1953.

—— 'Solo Song and Cantata', *The New Oxford History of Music*, vol. IV, Oxford, 1968.

Gabry, Gyorgy: *Old Musical Instruments*, Budapest, 1969.

Galpin, F. W.: *Old English Instruments of Music*, 4th. ed., revised by Thurston Dart, London, 1965.

Gavall, John: 'The Guitar – an Evaluation', *The Musical Times*, vol. xcv, November, 1954.

Geiringer, Karl: 'Der Instrumentenname "Quinterne" und die mittelalterliche Bezeichnungen der Gitarre, Mandola und Colascione', *Archiv für Musikwissenschaft VI*, 1924.

Gérard, Yves: *Thematic, Bibliographical and Critical Catalogue of the Works of Luigi Boccherini*, tr. Andreas Mayor, London, 1969.

Gill, Donald: 'James Talbot's Manuscript (Christ Church Library Music MS 1187), v. Plucked Strings – The Wirestrung fretted instruments and the Guitar', *Galpin Society Journal*, vol. XV, 1962.

Grunfeld, Frederic V.: *The Art and Times of the Guitar*, London, 1969.

Hamilton, Mary Neal: *Music in Eighteenth-Century Spain*, Illinois, 1937.

Harrison, Frank and Rimmer, Joan:

European Musical Instruments, London, 1964.

Harrison, Frank Mott: *Reminiscences of Madame Sidney Pratten, Guitariste and Composer*, London, 1899.

Haupt, Helga: *Wiener Instrumentenbauer von 1791 bis 1815*, Studien zur Musikwissenschaft, Beihefte der Denkmäler der Tonkunst in Österreich, vol. XXIV, 1960.

Hayes, Gerald: 'Instruments and Instrumental Notation', *The New Oxford History of Music*, Vol. IV, Oxford, 1968.

Heartz, Daniel: 'Les styles instrumentaux dans la musique de la Renaissance', *La Musique Instrumentale de la Renaissance*, ed. Jean Jacquot, Paris, 1955.

—— 'Parisian Music Publishing under Henry II a propos of four recently discovered guitar books', *The Musical Quarterly*, vol. XLVI, No. 4, 1960.

—— 'An Elizabethan Tutor for the Guitar', *Galpin Society Journal*, vol. XVII, 1964.

Heck, Thomas Fitzsimmons: *The Birth of the Classic Guitar and its Cultivation in Vienna, reflected in the Career and Compositions of Mauro Giuliani (d. 1829) (with) vol. II: Thematic Catalogue of the Complete Works of Mauro Giuliani*, Ph.D. dissertation, Yale University, 1970.

—— 'The role of Italy in the early history of the classic guitar', *Guitar Review*, 34, 1971.

—— Review of *The Art and Times of the Guitar* by Frederic V. Grunfeld and *The Illustrated History of the Guitar* by Alexander Bellow, *Journal of the American Musicological Society*, vol. XXIV, No. 2, 1971, pp. 310–313.

Hellwig, Günther: 'Joachim Tielke', *Galpin Society Journal*, vol. XVII, 1964.

Hipkins, A. J. and Gibb, W.: *Musical Instruments, Historic, Rare and Unique*, Edinburgh, 1888.

Hogarth, George: 'Musical Instruments – The Harp and Guitar', *The Musical World*, vol. III, No. 32, October 1836.

Hudson, Richard: 'The Concept of Mode in Italian Guitar Music during the First Half of the Seventeenth Century', *Acta Musicologica*, vol. XLII, 1970.

—— 'The *Zarabanda* and *Zarabanda Francese* in Italian Guitar Music of the Early 17th Century', *Musica Disciplina*, vol. XXIV, 1970.

—— 'The *Folia* Dance and the *Folia* Formula in 17th Century Guitar Music', *Musica Disciplina*, vol. XXV, 1971.

—— 'Further Remarks on the Passacaglia and Ciaconna', *Journal of the American Musicological Society*, vol. XXIII, No. 2, 1970.

Huttig, II, H. E.: 'The Guitar Maker and his Techniques', *Guitar Review* No. 28, May 1965.

Jacquot, Jean(ed.): *La Musique Instrumentale de la Renaissance*, Paris, 1955.

—— *Le Luth et sa Musique*, Paris, 1958.

Jaffee, Michael: 'Harmony in the Solo Guitar Music of Heitor Villa-Lobos', *Guitar Review* No. 29, 1966.

Jahnel, Franz: *Die Gitarre und ihr Bau*, Frankfurt am Main, 1963.

Johnson, L. G.: *General T. Perronet-Thompson*, London, 1957.

Keith, Richard: 'The Guitar Cult in the Courts of Louis XIV and Charles II', *Guitar Review* No. 26, 1962.

—— '"La Guitarre Royale": A study of the career and compositions of Francesco Corbetta', *Recherches sur la Musique Française Classique* vol. VI, 1966.

Kinsky, Georg: *A History of Music in Pictures*, London, 1930.

Kirkpatrick, Ralph: *Domenico Scarlatti*, Princeton, 1953.

Koczirz, Adolf: 'Die Gitarrekompositionen in Miguel de Fuenllanas Orphenica Lyra (1554)', *Archiv für Musikwissenschaft* vol. IV, 1922.

—— 'Die Fantasien des Melchior de Barberis für die siebensaitige Gitarre (1549)', *Zeitschrift für Musikwissenschaft* vol. IV, 1922.

—— 'Über die Fingernageltechnik bei Saiteninstrumenta', *Festschrift für Guido Adler*, Vienna, 1930.

Lesure, François: 'La Guitare en France au XVIe. Siècle', *Musica Disciplina* vol. IV, 1950.

—— 'La facture instrumentale à Paris au Seizième Siècle', *Galpin Society Journal* vol. VII, 1954 and vol. X, 1957.

—— and Thibault, G.: *Biographie des Éditions d'Adrien le Roy et Robert Ballard, 1551–1598*, Paris, 1955.

Lozano Gonzalez, Don Antonio: *La Música Popular, Religiosa y*

Dramática en Zaragoza desde el Siglo XVI hasta neustros dias, Saragossa, 1895.

Lütgendorff, Willibald Leo von: *Die Geigen- und Lautenmacher vom Mittelalter bis zur Gegenwart*, Frankfurt-am-Main, 1922.

Mahillon, Victor Charles: *Catalogue descriptif et analytique du Musée Instrumental du Conservatoire Royal de Musique de Bruxelles*, 5 vols., Ghent, 1893–1912.

Marcuse, Sibyl: *Musical Instruments: A Comprehensive Dictionary*, New York, 1966.

McLeod, Donald and Welford, Robert: *The Classical Guitar; Design and Construction*, Leicester and New Jersey, 1971.

Mersenne, Marin: *Harmonie Universelle (Paris, 1636): The Books on Instruments*, tr. R. E. Chapman, The Hague, 1957.

Mitjana, Rafael: 'La Musique en Espagne', *Encyclopédie de la Musique et Dictionnaire du Conservatoire*, Part I, vol. IV, Paris, 1920.

Murphy, Sylvia: 'Seventeenth-Century Guitar Music: Notes on Rasgueado Performance', *Galpin Society Journal*, vol. XXI, 1968.

—— 'The Tuning of the Five-course guitar', *Galpin Society Journal*, vol. XXIII, 1970.

Narkiss, Bezalel: *Hebrew Illuminated Manuscripts*, Jerusalem, 1969.

Nelson, Martha: 'Canarios', *Guitar Review* 25, 1961.

Newman, William S.: *The Sonata in the Classic Era*, Chapel Hill, 1963.

North, Roger: *Roger North on Music, being a selection from his* essays written during the years c. 1695–1728, transcribed and edited by John Whitridge Wilson, London, 1959.

Paganelli, Sergio: *Gli Strumenti musicali nell' arte*, Milan, 1966.

Pahissa, Jaime: *Manuel de Falla, his Life and Works*, tr. Jean Wagstaff, London, 1954.

Pierre, Constant: *Les Facteurs d'Instruments de Musique*, Paris, 1893.

Pirrotta, Nino: 'Music and Cultural Tendencies in fifteenth century Italy', *Journal of the American Musicological Society*, vol. XIX, No. 2, 1966.

Pohlmann, Ernst: *Laute, Theorbe, Chitarrone: die Instrumente, ihre Musik und Literatur von 1500 bis zur Gegenwart*, Bremen, 1968.

Pope, Isabel: 'La Vihuela y su Musica en el Ambiente Humanístico', *Nueva Revista de Filología Hispanica*, vol. XV, 1961.

Pope Conant, Isabel: 'Vicente Espinel as a Musician', *Studies in the Renaissance*, vol. V, 1958.

Poulton, Diana: 'Notes on some Differences between the Lute and the Vihuela and their Music', *The Consort*, No. 16, July, 1959.

—— 'Notes on the Spanish Pavan', *The Lute Society Journal*, vol. III, 1961.

Praetorius, Michael: *Syntagma musicum II De Organographia*, Wolffenbüttel, 1619, facsimile edition, Kassel, 1929.

Prat, Domingo: *Diccionario biografico, bibliografico, critico, de Guitarras, Guitarristas and Guitarreros*, Buenos Aires, 1934.

Prynne, Michael: 'A surviving Vihuela de Mano', *Galpin Society Journal*, vol. XVI, 1963.

Pujol, Emilio: 'La Guitare', *Encyclopédie de la Musique et Dictionnaire du Conservatoire*, Part II, vol. III, Paris, 1927.

—— *La Guitarra y su Historia, Conferencia*, Buenos Aires, 1932.

—— 'Significacion de Juan Carlos Amat (1572–1642) en la historia de la guitarra', *Anuario Musical* vol. V, 1950.

—— 'Les ressources instrumentales et leur rôle dans la musique pour vihuela et pour guitare au XVIe siècle et au XVIIe', *La Musique Instrumentale de la Renaissance*, ed. Jean Jacquot, Paris, 1958.

—— *Escuela Razonada de la Guitarra*, Book One, Buenos Aires, 1956.

—— *El Dilema del Sonida en la Guitarra*, Buenos Aires, 1960.

—— *Tárrega, Ensayo Biográfico*, Lisbon, 1960.

Pulver, Jeffrey: *A Dictionary of old English music and musical instruments*, London, 1923.

Ravizza, Victor: *Die Instrumentale Ensemble von 1400–1550 in Italien*, Bern and Stuttgart, 1970.

Riemann, Hugo: 'Das Lautenwerk des Miguel de Fuenllana 1554', *Monatshefte für Musikgeschichte*, vol. XXVII, No. 6, 1895.

Rimmer, Joan: Review of *The Illustrated History of the Guitar* by Alexander Bellow, *Notes*, vol. XXVII, 2 December 1970.

Roberts, John: 'Some Notes on the Music of the Vihuelistas', *The Lute Society Journal*, vol. VII, 1965.

—— 'The Death of Guzman', *The Lute Society Journal*, vol. X, 1968.

—— 'The flesh-nail controversy', *Guitar*, August, 1972.

—— 'Miguel Llobet', *Guitar*, vol. I, No. 5, December, 1972.

Rocamora, Manuel: *Fernando Sor (1778–1839), Ensayo Biográfico*, Barcelona, 1957.

Rothschild, Germaine de: *Luigi Boccherini, his Life and Work*, tr. Andreas Mayor, London, 1965.

Ruth-Sommer, Hermann: *Alte Musikinstrumente*, Berlin, 1920.

Sachs, Curt: *The History of Musical Instruments*, London, 1942.

—— *Real-Lexicon der Musikinstrumente*, 2nd. revised and enlarged ed., New York, 1964.

Salazar, Adolfo: 'Música, Instrumentos y Danzas en las Obras de Cervantes', *Nueva Revista de Filología Hispanica* II, 1948.

Sasser, William: *The Guitar Works of Fernando Sor*, unpublished Ph.D. dissertation, University of North Carolina, 1960.

—— 'In Search of Sor', *Guitar Review* 26, 1962.

Saussine, Renée de: *Paganini*, tr. Marjorie Laurie, New York, 1954.

Schmitz, Eugen: 'Über Guitarrentabulaturen', *Monatschefte für Musikgeschichte* XXXV No. 9, 1903.

Segovia, Andrés: 'Guitar Strings before and after Albert Augustine', *Guitar Review* 17, 1955.

Sharpe, A. P.: *The Story of the Spanish Guitar*, 3rd. ed., London, 1963.

Sherrington, Unity and Oldham, Guy (eds): *Music, Libraries and*

Instruments, Hinrichsen's 11th Music Book, London, 1961.

Sloane, Irving: *Classic Guitar Construction*, New York, 1966.

Smith, C. Colin (ed.): *Spanish Ballads*, Oxford, 1964.

Smith, Isabel: 'Performer's Platform –3: Letter from a Guitarist', *The Composer*, Autumn, 1967.

Stainer, J. R. F.: 'Lutes and Guitars', *Musical Times*, vol. XLI, 1900.

Stevens, Denis: *The Mulliner Book. A Commentary*, London, 1952.

Stevenson, Robert M.: *Music before the Classic Era*, London, 1952.

—— *Juan Bermudo*, The Hague, 1960.

Straeten, Edmund van der: *La Musique aux Pays Bas avant le XIXe siècle*, 8 vols., Brussels, 1867–1888.

Tappert, Wilhelm: 'Zur Geschichte der Guitarre', *Monatshefte für Musikgeschichte* vol. XIV, No. 5, 1882.

Thomas, Juan M.: 'The Guitar and its Renaissance', *The Chesterian*, VIII, 1927.

Tilmouth, Michael: 'Some Improvements in Music noted by William Turner in 1697', *Galpin Society Journal*, vol. X, 1957.

Tonazzi, Bruno: *Miguel Llobet, Chitarrista dell' Impressionismo*, Ancona and Milan, 1966.

Trend, J. B.: *Luis Milan and the Vihuelistas*, London, 1925.

—— *The Music of Spanish History to 1600*, London, 1926.

—— *Manuel de Falla and Spanish Music*, New York, 1929.

Trichet, Pierre: *Traité des instruments de musique c.1640*, ed. François Lesure, *Annales Musicologiques*, vol. III, 1955, and IV, 1956.

Usher, Terence: 'The Spanish Guitar in the Nineteenth and Twentieth Centuries', *Galpin Society Journal*, vol. XI, 1956.

Virdung, Sebastian: *Musica getutscht*, Basel, 1511; Facsimile edition, ed. Leo Schrade, Kassel, 1931.

Vol'man, Boris: *Gitara i Gitaristy: ocherk istorii shestistrunnoï gitary*, Leningrad, 1968.

—— *Gitara v Rossii: ocherk istorii gitarnogo iskusstva*, Leningrad, 1961.

Wade, Graham: 'The Guitar in Primary Education', *Making Music* No. 72, Spring, 1970.

Walker, Thomas: 'Ciaconna and Passacaglia: Remarks on their Origins and Early History', *Journal of the American Musicological Society*, vol. XXI, 1968.

Ward, John M.: 'The Editorial Methods of Venegas de Henestrosa', *Musica Disciplina*, vol. VI, 1952.

—— *The Vihuela de Mano and its Music 1536–1576*, unpublished Ph.D. dissertation, New York University, 1953.

—— 'Le problème des hauteurs dans la musique pour luth et vihuela au XVIe siècle', *Le Luth et sa Musique*, ed. Jean Jacquot, Paris, 1958.

—— 'Spanish Musicians in Sixteenth-Century England', *Essays in Musicology in Honour of Dragan Plamenac on his 70th Birthday*, eds. Gustave Reese and Robert J. Snow, Pittsburgh, 1969.

Weckerlin, Jean Baptiste Theodore: *Nouveau Musiciana: extraits d'ouvrages rares ou bizarres*, Paris, 1890.

Weller, Malcolm: 'Nails', *Guitar*, vol. 1, No. 7, February, 1973.

Wessely-Kropik, Helene: *Lelio Col-ista, ein römischer Meister vor Corelli*, Vienna, 1961.

Wolf, Johannes: *Handbuch der Notationskunde*, Leipzig, 1919.

Woodfill, Walter L.: *Musicians in English Society from Elizabeth to Charles I*, Princeton, 1953.

Zuth, Josef: *Handbuch der Laute und Gitarre*, Vienna, 1926.

—— *Simon Molitor und die Wiener Gitarristik*, Vienna, 1920.

Index

Abell, John, 50
Achillini, Giovanni Filoteo, 7, 140
 Pl. 7
Adelaide, Princess, 55
Agricola, Martin, 55
Aguado, Dionisio, 82, 84, 88, 100,
 102, 104
 Escuela de Guitarra, 63
 Tripodion, 74–5, 102
Alba, Duchess of, 83
Albeniz, Isaac, 107
Alonzo, 69
Altmira, 70
Amalia, Duchess of Weimar, 63
Amat, Juan Carlos, 13, 57
 Guitarra Española de cinco órdenes,
 41–3, 129n2, n3, 142 Pl. 31
An, Princess
 Lute Book, 54–5
Angel-lute, 55, 56
Angles, Higini, 130n7
Apel, Willi, 137n18
Arbeau, Thoinot,
 Orchésographie, 35, 36, 131n14
Arcadelt, Jacques, 29, 37
Arcas, Julian, 106
Arcos, Duke of, 28
Arias, Vicente, 78
Arnold, Malcolm
 Guitar Concerto, 117
Arran, Lord, 49
Artaria, Domenico, 85
Attavanti, Attavante degli, 7

Bach, Johann Sebastian,
 Chaconne, 109
 Lute Suites, 109
Baille, Louis, 133n28
Baines, Anthony, 127n2, 128n16,
 134n5, 135n8, n9, n20

Ballard, Robert, 34
Ballesteros, Antonio
 Obra para guitarra de seis órdenes, 63
Barberiis, Melchiore de, 32–3, 36,
 142 Pl. 30
Barbero, Marcelo, 78
Barbour, J. Murray, 16, 129n32
Bass-viol, 50
Beatrice, Princess, 101
Beckhaus, J.,
 harp-guitar, 73
Beethoven, Ludvig van, 85
Bellini, Vincenzo, 96
Benavente-Osuna, Marquis of, 83
Benedid, José, 65, 66, 69, 135n16,
 143 Pl. 35
Bennett, Alfred,
 Instructions for the Spanish Guitar, 90,
 Pl. 46
Berkeley, Lennox,
 Sonatina, 117, 119
 Songs of the Half-Light, 118
Berlioz, Hector, 87, 88
Bermudo, Juan, 12, 13, 14, 27, 28, 33,
 45, 81, 128n18, n21, 129n29,
 n30, n31, 130n2, n3, n4, n6,
 131n12, 136n37
Bessaraboff, Nicholas, 130n45
Bible, Bishop's, 40
Bible, Portuguese, 7
Binkley, Thomas, 135n17
Blovin, Julien, 56
Bobri, Vladimir, 135n10, 138n47, n6,
 139n7
Boccherini, Luigi, 83, 88, 89, 114
Bone, Philip J., 137n23
Bonner, Stephen, 134n4, 135n14,
 136n26
Bouchet, Robert, 79
Bourdelot, Pierre-Michon, 59–60

159

Index

Index

Falla, Manuel de, 110–11, 112
  Homenaje, 110, 122
  La Tertulia, 111
Fardino, Lorenzo, 57
Federhofer, Hellmut, 133n37
Ferdinand Maria, Elector of Bavaria, 55
Ferrandière, Fernando
  Arte de tocar la Guitarra, 134n2
Ferranti, Zani de, 87
Fétis, François Joseph, 92
Fezandat, Michel, 37
Fier, Jan B., 86
Figaro, Le, 94
Fissore, Robert, 130n43, 136n24, n27, n32
Flac, Philippe, 18
Fleta, Ignacio, 80
Foix, Germaine de, 24–5
folia, 45
Folies d'Espagne, 32
Fortune, Nigel, 44, 131n10, n5, 132n6
Foscarini, Giovanni Paolo, 57
  Il primo, secondo e terzo libro della Chitarra Spagnola, 45–6, 143 Pl. 31
Francisco, Seignio,
  Easie Lessons on the Guittar, 48
Frescobaldi, Gerolamo, 45, 109
Fretting
  enharmonic guitar, 75–6
  equal temperament, 15, 17, 76
  just intonation, 76
  La manière de bien et justement entoucher les lucs et guiternes, 15–16
  modern constant, 129n34
  Pythagorean tuning, 15, 16
  rule of the eighteenth, 16–17
  twelfth fret position, 23, 67
Fuenllana, Miguel de, 12
  Covarde cavallero, 34
  Crucifixus est, 34
  Fantasias (for guitar), 33–4
  Orphenica Lyra, 12, 14, 24, 26, 27, 28, 31, 33, 142 Pl. 30
  Passeavase el Rey Moro, 34

Gaforus, Franchinus, 7, 140 Pl. 5
Galignani's Messenger, 94

Galileo, Vicenzo,
  Dialogo della musica, 16
Gallegos, Don José,
  guitarpa, 74, Pl. 41
García, Enrique, 78
García, Miguel (Padre Basilio), 82, 83
García-Abrines, Luis, 57–8, 134n41
Gaultier, Anne, 46
Gavall, John, 125
Geiringer, Karl, 128n10
Gérard, Yves, 136n3
Gerhard, Roberto,
  Cantares, 118
Gibbons, Orlando, 45
Gill, Donald, 135n18
Giustiniani, Vincenzio,
  Discorse sopra la Musica de suoi tempi, 44
Giuliani, Emilia, 85, 86
Giuliani, Mauro, 1, 82, 85–6, 88, 89, 92, 96, 97, 98, 100
  Concertos, 90
  Op. 111, Part 2 No. 3, 104
  Op. 128, 105
  Sonata, 90
  Variations on Partant pour la Syrie, 90–1
Giulianiad, The, 92, 95–8
Graeffer, Anton, 86
Gombert, Nicolas, 28, 29
Gorlier, Simon,
  Le Troysieme Livre, 34–5
Granata, Giovanni Battista, 46, 54, 57
Granjon, Robert, 37
Grobert, 168
Guerau, Don Francisco
  Poema Harmonica, 59
Guerrero, Francisco, 141 Pl. 16
Guitar, related terms,
  biguela hordinaria, 56
  chitarra alla spagnuola, 43
  chitarriglia, 43
  ghiterne, 11
  gittar, 50
  guitarre 18, 128n16
  guiterne, 17, 18, 47, 128n16

Index

DATE DUE	
MAR 08 2011	
APR 0 6 2017	
11/30/20	